MEN-AT-ARMS SERIES

EDITOR: MARTIN WINDROW

Germany's Eastern Front Allies 1941-45

Text *by* PETER ABBOTT and NIGEL THOMAS

Colour plates by MIKE CHAPPELL

OSPREY PUBLISHING LONDON

Published in 1982 by
Osprey Publishing Ltd
Member company of the George Philip Group
12–14 Long Acre, London WC2E 9LP
© Copyright 1982 Osprey Publishing Ltd
Reprinted 1983, 1985, 1986, 1987

British Library Cataloguing in Publication Data
Abbott, Peter
    Germany's Eastern Front allies, 1941–45.—
(Men-at-Arms series; 131)
    1. World War, 1939–1945—Campaigns—Russia
I. Title   II. Thomas, Nigel   III. Series
940.54'21   D757.54

ISBN 0 85045 475 1

Filmset in Great Britain
Printed in Hong Kong

Author's Note

In spite of the flood of works on the Second World War,
the armies of Germany's East European Allies have
received little attention. This book is an attempt to fill
that gap. The general history of the war on the Russian
front and the political histories of the countries concerned have been well covered elsewhere, and infor-
mation on weapons and equipment is available in
specialist works, but details of the organization of the
smaller armies and divisional level orders of battle for
them are hard to find, and we have accordingly
concentrated on these.

Space does not permit of a full bibliography, but we
have used the 'World War II German Military Studies'
series and order of battle data from the German
archives; British and American Intelligence material;
Finnish, Hungarian and Rumanian language official
histories and other publications (including Vladescu's
work on Rumanian uniforms); together with books and
articles in German (notably by Adonyi, Emilian,
Forstmeier and Gosztony) and English (especially
Doyle and Kliment, Probst and Prieskop).

We would like to acknowledge the generous help
provided by Philip Buss MA, Karlheinz Bühler,
Monsignor Vitéz Gabor, Dr Friedrich Herrmann,
Charles Kliment, Dr Marc Landry, Franklyn G.
Prieskop, Henry Rüütel, Pierre Verheye, Steven
Zaloga, and the staffs of the Bundesarchiv, Koblenz;
the Finnish Embassy London; the Heeresgeschichtliches Museum, Vienna; the Imperial War Museum
and the School of Slavonic and East European Studies,
London. Much of our material derives ultimately from
their researches: any mistakes, however, are our own.

Introduction

The 1930s were a time of growing tension for the smaller states of Eastern Europe. Since the end of the First World War they had enjoyed an independence which most of them had not known for centuries, but this was now threatened by the growing power of Nazi Germany and Soviet Russia. Germany had territorial claims against her eastern neighbours and an interest in their economic resources, especially Rumania's oil. Russia wanted to recover Finland, the Baltic States, Eastern Poland and Rumanian Bessarabia, all of which had been Tsarist provinces in 1914.

Instead of combining for self defence, the East European states were bitterly divided. The nationalities were so intermingled that border disputes were inevitable. The Hungarians in particular were dedicated to the recovery of the territory they had lost to their neighbours in 1919. The 'Little Entente' of Czechoslovakia, Yugoslavia and Rumania was a defensive alliance against Hungarian ambitions; but even this relatively stable grouping contained a fatal division of interest, for the Rumanians feared the Russians more than the Germans, and when Hitler threatened Czechoslovakia in 1939 they refused to allow Russian troops to cross their territory to help the Czechs. The Munich crisis also showed how little reliance could be placed on the Western democracies, whose power to intervene militarily in Eastern Europe was negligible. In effect this left the smaller East European states with little alternative but to become clients of either Germany or Russia.

The German and Russian leaders saw this clearly, and one of the main purposes of the Russo-German Pact of 1939 was to divide up Eastern Europe into spheres of influence. The Russians claimed Bessarabia, East Poland, the Baltic States and Finland, and immediately began to consolidate their position. Only the Finns were able to preserve their independence, and even they lost substantial amounts of territory at the end of the Winter War of 1939–40.

The Germans were faced with the problem of keeping the peace within their sphere of influence. The Hungarians claimed a slice of the newly established puppet state of Slovakia, and used force to obtain it. The Slovaks had claims of their own against Poland, and pursued these by joining in the German attack. Then, in 1940, the Hungarians threatened to go to war with Rumania over Transylvania. The Vienna Award of August

Instructor at the Light Services Combat School supervises practice with the Suomi sub-machine gun; Finland, autumn 1939 (S. Zaloga)

1940 allotted half of the disputed territory to the Hungarians, who then went on to establish their claims to the Banat by participating in the attack on Yugoslavia in April 1941.

The end result of these changes was to exacerbate national hatreds while at the same time tying all the countries concerned more closely to Germany. Rumania's only hope of recovering her lost lands lay in such an alliance; Slovakia's security depended upon German 'protection'; while Hungary stood to lose her considerable gains if she fell out with her powerful friend. All three joined the Tripartite Pact in 1940, along with Bulgaria. Finland remained uncommitted in theory, but allowed free passage across her soil to German troops, and entered into joint military discussions. Hitler counted on the support of both the Finns and the Rumanians in his 'Barbarossa' planning, and they were undoubtedly told of his intentions in advance. Slovakia was actually the first satellite state to declare war on Russia, while Hungary joined in after a somewhat mysterious air raid had provided a convenient excuse. Only the traditionally pro-Russian Bulgarians managed to remain uninvolved.

Politically, the satellites had little in common with Nazi Germany. Finland was a parliamentary democracy; Hungary a monarchy with a vacant throne and a democratic, if right wing, government; and Rumania, a monarchy with a military ruler who had just suppressed his country's native Fascist Party. In fact, the Fascists in both Rumania and Hungary were to receive little or no help from the Germans until late in the war, when they were called in to provide puppet administrations after the legitimate governments had defected. Only Slovakia had a fully fledged totalitarian regime, and even that had a clerical bias very different from National Socialism. The only thing that these very different administrations had in common was an overriding fear of Russia and Communism.

* * *

The satellite contribution to the war in the east can be divided into five phases. During the first stages of 'Barbarossa' strong Finnish and Rumanian forces advanced alongside the Germans, together with smaller representative contingents from Hungary, Italy and Slovakia. Once the Finns had reached their 1939 frontier they dug in and refused to go any further. The other national contingents were exhausted by the beginning of winter 1941–42, and the Hungarians and most of the Rumanians were withdrawn for regrouping.

The Germans, realising that they needed more men for their 1942 offensive, sent Field Marshal Keitel to persuade the Hungarians and Rumanians to provide more troops. Keitel had to agree to these forces serving as independent national armies. They began to arrive at the front during the summer of 1942. As the Germans fought their way into Stalingrad their allies found themselves holding long stretches of the Don front. The Russians saw their opportunity. In November 1942 they smashed through two Rumanian armies to encircle Stalingrad, then followed up with a series of hammer blows which destroyed the Italian and Hungarian armies.

'I never want to see another soldier of our Eastern Allies on the Eastern Front.' said Hitler after these disasters; and most of the survivors were indeed sent home at the beginning of 1943. The remainder were employed on anti-partisan and coast defence duties for the rest of the year. Their morale deteriorated, and their governments began to put out peace feelers to the Allies.

1944 saw the break-up of the Axis alliance. Early in the year the Rumanians had to come back into the line to stabilize the situation in the south, while the Slovaks and Hungarians prepared to defend the Carpathians against the advancing Russians. During August the Russians shattered the Rumanians once again and cut off another German army. The Rumanians then changed sides, and the Slovaks staged an unsuccessful revolt. Meanwhile, in the north, the Russians had launched an offensive against the Finns, who sued for peace and agreed to drive the Germans out of their country.

The final phase of the war thus saw the Rumanians and Finns actively engaged against the Germans, and Slovakia as an occupied country. Only Hungary remained at Germany's side, and that largely because a German coup had installed a Fascist government. The fact that the Rumanians were now in the opposite camp had some effect on the Hungarians, too, for the two countries shared a mutual hatred and, indeed, seem to have fought each other with noticeably more enthusiasm than either had shown against the Russians.

* * *

In late 1942, when their involvement was at its greatest, the satellite armies provided about a quarter of the Axis divisions on the Eastern Front. Apart from the Finns they were concentrated almost entirely in Army Group South. However, their deficiencies in equipment, training and motivation meant that their presence in the line was a source of weakness. By the closing stages of

Marshal Mannerheim leaves the Finnish Parliament building after being elected President, 4 August 1944. His sleeve badge is that of the Civil Guard. (Finnish Embassy, London)

the war the Germans had lost all enthusiasm for masses of unwilling allied conscripts and were looking only for limited numbers of fanatical recruits who could be organized and equipped along German lines. Nevertheless, they admit that the Finns were supreme in their own northern theatre of operations, and that Hungarians, Italians, Rumanians and Slovaks fought well on many occasions.

Relations between the Germans and their allies seem to have been generally good. Many of the latters' senior officers had previous experience of working with the Germans. The Hungarians and Slovaks had fought beside them in the Austro-Hungarian army during the First World War, often against the Russians; and many of the Finns had served in the German army as part of a volunteer Jäger battalion. Their respect for German military abilities helped them to accept 'advice' from German liaison officers, though the traditional terseness of German staff communications sometimes offended those, like the Italians and Rumanians, who were used to more ceremonious language.

A factor of some importance, in view of Nazi racial theories, was that apart from the Slovaks none of the satellites were Slavs. The Finns and the Hungarians were racially quite distinct, and the Rumanians regarded themselves as the Latins of Eastern Europe. The Finns actually provided one of the earliest volunteer units of the Waffen-SS, even though the Germans appear to have thought initially that it would consist mainly of 'Swedish' (Germanic) Finns. Race did, however, create one awkward problem. Scattered throughout Eastern Europe were colonies of Volksdeutsche or racial Germans, many of whom were proud of their ancestry and anxious to serve in German units. Those living in occupied territory presented no problem, since they could volunteer directly; but those in Hungary, Rumania and Slovakia were technically citizens of allied states and liable for service in their own armies. Since they were in the main relatively well educated, their loss would have been a severe blow, especially to the technical services. Nevertheless, pressure from the Volksdeutsche themselves, and from the recruit-hungry Waffen-SS, combined to force Slovakia in 1940, Rumania in 1943 and Hungary in 1944 into

agreements allowing all Volksdeutsche other than specialists to volunteer for service in the German forces. Many had already done so illegally.

The satellite armies were far from being carbon copies of the Wehrmacht. They had their own traditions, organization and weapons. Austro-Hungarian influence was strong, along with French and, to a lesser extent, Italian. The Slovaks preserved the doctrines of the highly professional Czechoslovakian army, while the Finns had developed special tactics and weapons to suit their own unique circumstances. These differences created problems, since a satellite division was not necessarilly equivalent to a German one in terms of either numbers of fire-power. However, German influence did bring about a certain degree of standardization as the war went on, especially in the case of the armoured formations.

The most serious weakness of the satellite armies lay in their equipment. The East European states had little industrial capacity of their own, and once the war had begun they found it difficult to obtain supplies of heavy weapons. As a result they went to war with outmoded artillery, obsolete tanks, inadequate transport and even, in the case of Hungary, insufficient rifles. They were particularly short of anti-tank weapons, a weakness that the Russians were quick to exploit. The Germans tried to help by providing booty weapons captured from the Poles, French and Belgians, but these were all of obsolete pre-war patterns, and relatively few modern weapons were supplied. Moreover, German policy was curiously short-sighted, in that they insisted on payment in full for any arms deliveries. Indeed, when the Hungarians sought permission to manufacture the excellent 'Panther' tank in 1944, the deal fell through because the Germans demanded a prohibitively high price for the production rights. It is true that in 1942–43 the Germans initiated a study of weapons standardisation, and even reached a measure of argreement with the Hungarians, but in general little progress was made in this vital area.

The Allies had faced a similar problem in Tunisia when their troops were joined by the brave but ill-equipped units of the Armée d'Afrique. The French were given mountainous

Territorial Changes in Eastern Europe 1938–41
- – · – · 1938 Frontiers
- To Germany
- To U.S.S.R.
- To Bulgaria
- To Hungary
- To Italy
- To Slovakia

NORWAY

SWEDEN

FINLAND

Karelia

DENMARK

BALTIC SEA

ESTONIA

LATVIA

LITHUANIA

GERMANY

GERMANY

POLAND

U.S.S.R.

CZECHO-SLOVAKIA

AUSTRIA

Ruthenia

Bukovina

HUNGARY

Transylvania

Bessarabia

Croatia

Backa

RUMANIA

ITALY

YUGOSLAVIA

Dobruja

BLACK SEA

BULGARIA

ALBANIA

Macedonia

Thrace

GREECE

TURKEY

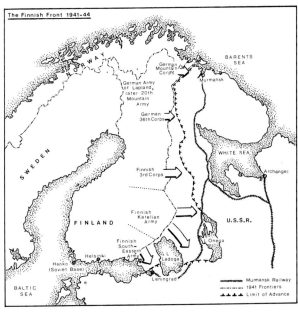

The Finnish Front 1941–44

NORWAY

BARENTS SEA

German Mountain Corps

German Army of Lapland, later 20th Mountain Army

Murmansk

SWEDEN

German 36th Corps

WHITE SEA

Archangel

Finnish 3rd Corps

Finnish Karelian Army

Onega

FINLAND

Finnish South-Eastern Army

U.S.S.R.

Hanko (Soviet Base)

Helsinki

L. Ladoga

Leningrad

BALTIC SEA

- ┿┿┿┿ Murmansk Railway
- – · – · 1941 Frontiers
- ▲▲▲▲ Limit of Advance

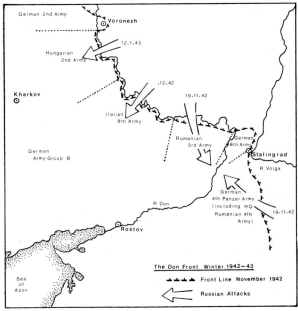

German 2nd Army

Voronezh

12.1.43

Hungarian 2nd Army

Kharkov

.12.42

19.11.42

Italian 8th Army

German 6th Army

Rumanian 3rd Army

Stalingrad

German Army Group B

R Volga

German 4th Panzer Army (including HQ Rumanian 4th Army)

19.11.42

R Don

Rostov

The Don Front Winter 1942–43

- ▲▲▲ Front Line November 1942
- ⬅ Russian Attacks

Sea of Azov

7

Finnish officers and an NCO in a Karelian forest, early 1944,
Most wear the obsolete khaki M1927 tunic with its distinctive
skirt pockets. (Finnish Embassy, London)

Finland

sectors to hold in the hope that these would provide protection against the Panzers, but the Germans still broke through. Thereafter all Allied contingents were equipped up to British or American standards, and this source of weakness was eliminated. This was made possible by America's immense industrial capacity. The Germans were unable to meet their own requirements, let alone those of their smaller allies. This meant that the satellite forces were always weak links in the line of defence. Brave though the men were, they could not be expected to go on fighting forever as 'poor relations' in a cause which was clearly lost.

Until 1917 Finland formed part of the Russian Empire. Then the Finns, aided by German troops, established their independence. During the inter-war years they pursued a policy of neutrality, but remained fearful that the Russians would one day attempt to reconquer their former province. In October 1939 the Soviet government suddenly demanded a military base at Hanko, together with territorial concessions in eastern Finland. Faced with overwhelming Soviet military superiority the Finns attempted to negotiate; but on 30 November, without even declaring war, Soviet forces attacked along the entire length of the Finnish border. The 'Winter War' had begun.

Initially the three peacetime Finnish divisions (1st to 3rd) were broken up to form the nuclei of eight infantry divisions numbered 4th to 6th, 8th and 10th to 13th. The 6th, 10th and 11th were later renumbered 2nd, 3rd and 7th respectively. Later the 1st, 9th, 21st and 23rd Divs. were added, making a total of twelve. A division had 15,000 men, organised in three infantry regiments (each with three battalions), an artillery regiment with only 36 obsolete guns, and a reconnaissance unit with a mounted squadron, a motorcycle company and a sub-machine gun battalion. The tank arm comprised Independent Tank Companies 1 to 5 with 59 obsolete Vickers 'E' and Renault tanks, but only the 4th Company was to see action. Seventeen para-military Civic Guard battalions and five élite Frontier Guard units covered the eastern frontier. The whole army possessed only 112 Bofors 37mm anti-tank guns and 100 Bofors anti-aircraft guns, the latter reserved for home defence. With 120,000 troops facing 300,000 Russians with 1,500 tanks, the Finns were superior only in warm winter clothing and their unrivalled fighting spirit.

Field Marshal Mannerheim's strategy was to concentrate his Karelian Army of 2nd Corps (4th, 5th, 6th and 11th Divs.) and 3rd Corps (8th and 9th Divs.) on the Mannerheim Line spanning the vital Karelian isthmus. 4th Corps (12th and 13th Divs.) was north of Lake Ladoga, with 5th Corps and Lapland Force covering the central and northern sectors. At first Finnish infantry tactics carried the day as independent battle groups on skis and armed with Suomi submachine guns attacked floundering Russian columns, destroying stranded enemy tanks at night with Molotov cocktails. Miraculously, the Soviet advance was stopped, and at Suomussalmi two entire Russian divisions were wiped out.

However, by February 1940 relentless pressure finally opened a breach in the Mannerheim Line. As their troops slowly gave ground, the Finnish government sued for peace, and in March they reluctantly conceded the Soviet demands. The Finnish army was exhausted, though it had emerged from its ordeal rich in experience and prestige.

The following year Finland, convinced that a new Soviet invasion was only a matter of time, was drawn into partnership with Germany, though this never became a formal alliance. Although they accepted military and economic aid from

Lieutenant Esa Seeste, former Finnish Olympic athlete, in Karelia July 1941, wearing the summer tunic and his field cap under the M1917 helmet. His rank devices are pinned directly to his collar. (Signal)

1942: a Finnish gun crew in summer field uniform with a mixture of Czech M1934, German M1917 and Italian M1933 helmets. (Finnish Embassy, London)

Germany, the Finns made it clear that their only objective in joining in an attack on Russia would be to recover the territory ceded after the Winter War.

In May 1940 the Finnish army was re-organised to create sixteen infantry divisions. The 1939 divisional structure was retained, but the infantry regiments were re-allocated to give each division a regular regiment (1st to 16th), to be joined on mobilisation by two reserve regiments (normally adding 21 and 42 to the number of the regular regiment). Thirteen divisions were stationed along the border. Seven naval coast artillery brigades guarded the coastline. Finland's élite mobile troops included the Cavalry Brigade, which operated as mounted infantry in summertime and as ski troops in winter, and which was in process of being motorised, plus two Jäger Brigades with infantry mounted on lorries or bicycles. The field and anti-tank artillery had been greatly strengthened by an influx of German and booty

material. Signals equipment remained poor, however. The infantry retained their Russian-designed 7.62mm Mosin Nagant rifles, together with the superb Suomi. The tank force was expanded to three battalions with the aid of captured Soviet T-26s, T-37s and T-38s.

The Finns called their participation in the Russo-German war the 'Continuation War'. The country was divided into the Southern (Finnish) and Northern (German) Fronts. The South-Eastern Army, with 2nd Corps (2nd, 10th, 15th and 18th Divs. plus 2nd Coast Artillery Bde.) and 4th Corps (4th, 8th and 17th Divs.) advanced into the Karelian isthmus. It halted in early September 1941 only 30 miles from Leningrad, having recaptured all the lost Finnish territory. The Karelian Army, with 6th Corps (1st, 5th and 11th Finnish plus 163rd German Divs., and 1st Jäger Bde.), 7th Corps (7th and 19th Divs.) and the Oinen Group (the Cavalry and 2nd Jäger Bde.) advanced east of Lake Ladoga into Soviet territory; but by September it too had halted, along the River Svir. Operations further north were less successful. By August 3rd Corps (3rd Div. only) had made some headway, but was unable to achieve its goal of cutting the strategically vital Murmansk railway. Even this modest advance outshone the performance of the German 36th Corps (which included the Finnish 6th Div.) and Mountain Corps in the far north, for they had scarcely moved at all.

By December 1941 Germany's failure to capture Moscow had put her ultimate victory in doubt. Finland could not afford the heavy losses and economic disruption of a protracted campaign, so Mannerheim decided to stabilise the front. The Germans were furious but had to accept that their troops, ill-suited to the endless snows and depressing gloom of the Lapland winter, could not operate without the stoical and resolute Finns. The Finns, who were invited to train the Germans in winter warfare and forest fighting, openly despised their comrades in arms, believing that they depended too much on mechanisation at the expense of individual initiative.

The front was to remain virtually static until June 1944. In the meantime a battalion of Finns had served with the Waffen-SS in the Ukraine, but in June 1943 Mannerheim insisted that they return to rejoin the Finnish army. A Swedish volunteer battalion helped the Finns, as did a number of Estonian refugees, who formed, in February 1944, the 200th Infantry Regiment. An Armoured Division was organised in August 1943, comprising two tank 'brigades' with a total of 150 tanks—mainly captured T-26s—an assault gun 'brigade' with Bt-42s and German Sturmgeschütz IIIs, a Jäger brigade and supporting services.

On 9 June 1944 half a million Soviet troops with 800 tanks attacked 3rd and 4th Corps on the Karelian isthmus. 4th Corps' 10th Div. took the full brunt of the onslaught and suffered heavy casualties, but the Finns fought back skilfully in a rearguard action which saw the most intensive fighting of the war. Mannerheim begged Hitler for aid and promptly received a German infantry division, an assault gun brigade and large quantities of Panzerfaust and Panzerschreck anti-tank weapons. 5th Corps was transferred to the Karelian front, and the Armoured Division was thrown in to stop the Soviet advance, pitting its obsolete T-26s against the enemy T-34s. By the end of June the Finns had been forced back to the

post-1940 frontier, where they succeeded in digging in. Meanwhile more Soviet troops attacked over the River Svir and slowly pushed back 2nd and 6th Corps, weakened by the transfer of 5th Corps, along the eastern shores of Lake Ladoga. By the end of June they too had dug in along the old frontier. All the gains of the 'Continuation War' had been lost.

Mannerheim was now determined to take Finland out of the war; and on 25 August 1944 he concluded an alliance with Moscow, agreeing to expel the German forces in Lapland from Finnish soil. The Germans bowed reluctantly to Finnish wishes, and by the end of 1944 had withdrawn into northern Norway after some local skirmishes with Finnish forces (the 1st, 3rd, 6th, 11th and Armoured Divs. were involved in following up the German withdrawal).

Tiny Finland had managed to field an army of 400,000 men and had lost 55,000 killed. The country's economy was in ruins; but the sacrifices of its people and the courage with which its

Early 1944: Estonian officers of the Finnish 200th Inf. Regt.; all wear Finnish uniform, but note the blue-black-white Estonian arm shield worn by the fourth officer from the right. (Henry Rüütel)

soldiers, faced with overwhelming odds, had preserved it from Soviet occupation.

The 1941 Divisional Order of Battle was as follows:

1st Inf.—14,35,56,60 Inf, 5 Art. Regts.; 8 Recce Bde.

2nd Inf.—7,28,49 Inf., 15 Art. Regts.; 7 Recce Bde.

3rd Inf.—11,32,53 Inf.; 16 Art. Regts.; 5 Recce Bde.

4th Inf.—5,25,46 Inf., 1 Art. Regts.; 9,14 Recce Bdes.

5th Inf.—2,23,44 Inf. 3 Art. Regts.; 4 Recce Bde.

6th Inf.—12,33,54 Inf., 14 Art. Regts.; 3 Recce Bde.

7th Inf.—9,30,51 Inf., 2 Art. Regts., 15 Recce Bde.

8th Inf.—4,24,45 Inf., 11 Art. Regts.

10th Inf.—1,22,43 Inf., 9 Art. Regts.; 12 Recce Bde.

11th Inf.—8,29,50 Inf., 4 Art. Regts.; 10 Recce Bde.

12th Inf.—3,26,47,55 Inf., 7 Art. Regts.; 1 Recce Bde.

14th Inf.—10,31,53 Inf., 18 Art. Regts.; 2 Recce Bde.

15th Inf.—15,36,57 Inf., 12 Art. Regts.; 16 Recce Bde.

17th Inf.—13,34 Inf., 8 Art. Regts.; 19 Recce Bde.

18th Inf.—6,27,48 Inf., 19 Art. Regts.; 6 Recce Bde.

19th Inf.—16,37,58,61 Inf., 10 Art. Regts.; 18 Recce Bde.

Armoured (1943)—I,II Tank Bdes., Assault Gun Bde.; Jäger Bde. (2,3,4,5 Bns.); 14 Art. Bn., AT Bn.

Hungary

The Treaty of Trianon in 1920 reduced the Kingdom of Hungary, now under Regent Miklos Horthy, Vice-Admiral and last commander-in-chief of the Austro-Hungarian Navy, to one third of its former area and population. It permitted her a regular army of only 35,000 men, divided into seven mixed brigades, headquarters troops and a small Danube Naval Flotilla; and prohibited tanks, heavy artillery and an air force.

Hungary's principal foreign policy objective was to regain her lost territories. She developed close links with Italy, and then, increasingly, with Germany. In 1939 she began to re-arm. The brigades (an 8th had just been formed) were expanded to Army Corps, a Mobile Corps and an Air Force were created and the covert system of conscription was made official.

Hungary regained southern Slovakia as part of the 1938 Munich settlement. In March 1939 her forces (8th and Mobile Corps) occupied Czechoslovakian Ruthenia, and in August 1940 the Germans forced Rumania to hand back northern Transylvania. Hungary's eastern frontier was now on the strategically important Carpathians; but Rumania had become a bitter enemy, and it was necessary to maintain a large garrison in the new 9th (Carpathian) Corps area. In April 1941 Hungarian forces (including the Mobile Corps and the newly formed Parachute Company) occupied certain disputed Yugoslavian districts in the wake of the German invasion. Hungary had now regained much of her lost territory, but at the cost of alienating all her non-German neighbours and becoming totally dependent on German backing.

At this period the country was divided into nine corps areas. Each raised three 'Dandár' or Light Divisions, not unlike the Italian binary divisions. They had one first-line and one corresponding reserve infantry regiment, each of three battalions; a two-battalion artillery regiment with 24 guns; a cavalry troop, and anti-aircraft and signals companies. The regimental heavy weapons platoons and companies contained some 38 anti-tank rifles and 40 anti-tank guns, mainly 37mm calibre. Each Corps had a lorried infantry battalion (in

Officer cadets of the Hungarian Ludowika Academy with their Ansaldo tankettes, probably in 1941. Note the Czech tank overalls and the special cadet collar patches. The white-edged cross was red. (Martin Windrow)

practice, mounted on bicycles), and anti-aircraft, engineer and signals battalions. There were in addition two Mountain and eleven Border Guard brigades; numerous labour battalions raised from Jews and other minorities; and small Life Guard, Crown Guard and Parliament Guard units in Budapest. The Order of Battle was:

1st Cps.—1st Div. (1,31 Inf. Regts.), 2nd Div. (2 Inf. Regt.)

2nd Cps.—4th Div. (3,33 Inf. Regts.), 5th Div. (16,46 Inf. Regts.), 6th Div. (22,52 Inf. Regts).

3rd Cps.—7th Div. (4,34 Inf. Regts.), 8th Div. (5,35 Inf. Regts.), 9th Div. (17, 47 Inf. Regts.)

4th Cps.—10th Div. (6,36 Inf. Regts.), 11th Div. (8,38 Inf. Regts.), 12th Div. (18,48 Inf. Regts.)

5th Cps.—13th Div. (7,37 Inf. Regts.), 14th Div. (9,39 Inf. Regts.), 15th Div. (20,50 Inf. Regts.)

6th Cps.—16th Div. (10,40 Inf. Regts.), 17th Div. (11,41 Inf. Regts.), 18th Div. (19,49 Inf. Regts.)

7th Cps.—19th Div. (13,43 Inf. Regts.), 20th Div. (14,44 Inf. Regts.), 21st Div. (23,53 Inf. Regts.)

8th Cps.—22nd Div. (12,42 Inf. Regts.), 23rd Div. (21,51 Inf. Regts.), 24th Div. (24,54 Inf. Regts.)

9th Cps.—25th Div. (25,55 Inf. Regts.), 26th Div. (26,56 Inf. Regts.), 27th Div. (27,57 Inf. Regts.)

Mobile—1st Mot. Bde. (1,2,3 Mot. Inf., 9,10 Cycle, 1 Recce Bns., 1 Mot. Art. Grp.); 2nd Mot. Bde. (4,5,6 Mot. Inf., 11,12 Cycle, 2 Recce Bns., 2 Mot. Art. Grp.); 1st Cav. Bde. (3,4 Cav. Regts., 13,14 Cycle Bns., 1 Cav. Mot. Art. Grp.); 2nd Cav. Bde. (1,2 Cav. Regts., 15,16 Cycle Bns., 2 Cav. Mot. Art. Grp.)

Men of an artillery battery of the Hungarian 2nd Army, Russia, 1942. The commanding officer (centre front) is a lieutenant, and most of the other 'officers' are in fact cadets. (Vitez Gabor)

In practice many of these units remained at cadre strength only until 1944.

Although some modern equipment had been obtained, many of the weapons were First World War models, and even rifles were in short supply. The standard infantry weapons consisted of modified 8mm Mannlicher rifles and Solothurn and Schwarzlose machine guns. The calibre was changed to the German 7.92mm in 1943 in the interests of standardisation. The original German 37mm and Belgian 47mm anti-tank guns gave place to heavier German weapons as the war went on. The artillery used Skoda mountain and field guns, and Skoda, Bofors and Rheinmetall howitzers. The élite Mobile Corps was forced to requisition private cars and tractors to supplement its obsolete Italian tankettes and Hungarian-made Csaba armoured cars and Toldi light tanks.

Hungary had no quarrel with the Soviet Union, but Horthy felt obliged to help the Germans in order to ensure the retention of Transylvania. Even so, he thought it wise to keep the bulk of his army at home to deter the Rumanians; when Hungary declared war on Russia on 27 June 1941, only a relatively small contingent actually joined the Axis forces. It was known as the 'Carpathian Group' and consisted of the 1st Mountain and 8th Frontier Bde., together with the Mobile Corps minus the 2nd Cav. Bde. It advanced into Soviet-occupied Galicia and on across the Dneister. Then the Mobile Corps pushed on alone into the Ukraine as part of the German 17th Army. It fought well at Uman, though it had to be held back from entering Nikolayev because there were Rumanian troops there. In October it reached the Donets after a spectacular 600-mile advance which had left 80 per cent of its motorised equipment behind in the Ukrainian mud. The cavalry, too, were exhausted, and in November the Corps was withdrawn to Hungary and disbanded.

The Germans had been impressed by the

Mobile Corps in spite of its defective equipment. German-Hungarian relations were good, as many senior Hungarian officers were either Volksdeutsche or German-speaking veterans of the Austro-Hungarian army. However, no love was lost between Horthy and Hitler. The German dictator, who had once praised the Hungarians as 'a nation of daring cavalrymen', had become disillusioned by their hatred for their 'allies' the Rumanians, and by their obvious desire to extract as much as they could from the alliance at minimal cost to themselves.

After September 1941 the 1st Mountain and 8th Border Brigades in Galicia were replaced by newly formed Security Divisions numbered 102, 105, 108, 121 and 124 ('100' was added to the parent division's number, though the battalions were drawn from all the Corps districts to equalize the burden). Designed to save manpower and equipment for the Home Army, each had only two reserve infantry regiments armed with light weapons, an artillery battery and a weak cavalry squadron, with a total strength of 6,000 men. In 1943 the artillery and reconnaissance elements were expanded to battalion strength. These formations were effectively only brigades, but they were often called upon to perform tasks requiring full divisions. In February 1942, for instance, the Germans put the 108th Security Division into the line at Kharkov, where it was badly mauled. Normally they were grouped into 8th Corps (soon known to the Hungarians as the 'Dead Army'), based at Kiev and responsible for guarding communications in the North-East Ukraine against attacks by Polish, Soviet and Ukrainian partisans. The Germans suspected them of fraternising too readily with the local population: the Hungarians were appalled by the German massacres of the Jews and stopped them when they could.

In spring 1942 Germany's need for more manpower on the Eastern Front led the Hungarians to mobilize their 2nd army, with 200,000 men organised as follows:

3rd Cps.—6th Div. (22,52 Inf. Regts.), 7th Div. (4,35 Inf. Regts.), 9th Div. (17,47 Inf. Regts.)
4th Cps.—10th Div. (6,36 Inf. Regts.), 12th Div. (18,48 Inf. Regts.), 13th Div. (7,37 Inf. Regts.)
7th Cps.—19th Div. (13,43 Inf. Regts.), 20th Div.

A Hungarian anti-tank gun on the Don front, summer 1942. The crew are in shirt sleeve order and most wear M1917 helmets, except for the loader, who has the more compact M1938. (Vitez Gabor)

A Hungarian Huszár of the Mobile Corps, summer 1941. Note the distinctive cap flash with its three braids, and the field collar patch. (Vitez Gabor)

(14,23 Inf. Regts.), 23rd Div. (21,51 Inf. Regts.)
Army Units—1st Armoured Div. (30 Armd. and 1 Mot. Inf. Regts., 1 Recce and 51 AT. Bns.) plus 101 Hvy. Art., 150 Mot. Art., 101 Mot. AA. Art. and 151 Eng. Bns.

Each division had an artillery regiment and service units bearing the divisional number. After October 1942 each of the Light Divisions added a reconnaissance battalion formed from the newly organized Mobile Troops arm, which grouped together cavalry, motorised, cyclist and armoured units. The Armoured Division had been formed in spring 1942 from the two motorised brigades, and was equipped with PzKpfw 38(t), III and IV tanks as well as Hungarian Toldi light tanks, Csaba armoured cars and Nimrod self-propelled guns.

Russia, 1942: Hungarian troops breakfast off cow's milk. The soldier on the right wears the green, brown and ochre Hungarian camouflage cape. (Vitez Gabor)

Commanded by Gen. Jany, the 2nd Army reached the front at Kursk in June 1942, and advanced to hold a defensive line along the Don south of Voronezh. It held this sector against Soviet raids across the river, but by the end of 1942 its morale and efficiency had deteriorated in the harsh winter conditions. The Germans complained that the Hungarians were reluctant to engage the enemy, and added that the army was understrength and poorly equipped. The Hungarians, for their part, repeatedly begged the Germans to provide them with modern anti-tank weapons to supplement their obsolete 20mm and 37mm guns, which were useless against T-34 tanks.

On 12 January 1943 Soviet tanks crossed the frozen Don and tore through the 7th and 12th Divs.' defences. The 1st Armd. Div. was held back under German tactical control and was not allowed to counter-attack in time to save the situation. The army retreated in disorder, briefly protected by a brave rearguard action by 3rd Corps. Some 30,000 men were lost, together with almost all the tanks and heavy weapons, while another 50,000 were taken prisoner. It was the worst disaster in Hungarian military history, and German-Hungarian relations reached an all-time low. The Hungarians accused the Germans of abandoning them to the Russians, and also of attacking the Jews in the labour battalions. The Germans were appalled by the suddenness of the 2nd Army's collapse and wanted no more Hungarians in the front line.

In March Horthy ordered the 2nd Army back to Hungary to strengthen the Home Army. Most of its reserve regiments were re-allocated to the 'Dead Army', however, which once again constituted the only Hungarian force actively engaged against the enemy. Its units were reshuffled and renumbered, a process which seems to have been intended to confuse the Germans as much as the Russians, and now comprised 8th Corps (5th, 9th, 12th and 23rd Divs.), based in White Russia, and 7th Corps (1st, 18th, 19th, 21st and 201st Divs.), which remained in the Ukraine.

In mid-1943 the Hungarians decided to reorganise their infantry divisions along German lines, with three infantry regiments each, and either three or four artillery battalions plus reconnaissance and engineer battalions. Each Corps' first line infantry regiments were grouped into 'Mixed Divisions', its reserve regiments into 'Reserve Divisions'. 1st Corps was made responsible for all the Mobile Troops, its main formations being the reconstituted 1st Armd. Div., the recently formed 2nd Armd. Div. and the 1st Cav. Div., formed in 1942 from the old cavalry brigades. The new Order of Battle was:

1st Cps. — 1 Armd. Div. (1 Armd., 1 Mot. Inf.

July 1944: a Frontier Guard of the Hungarian 1st Army in the Carpathians watches for signs of the forthcoming Soviet offensive. (Vitez Gabor)

Hungarian troops manhandle a PaK 38 50mm anti-tank gun, summer 1942. In the background is a PzKpfw 38(t) tank, probably in Hungarian service—the colour scheme would be brown and green camouflage, and the cross insignia in red outlined with white. The man second from right is seen to wear the characteristic gaiter-trousers; centre is a corporal, whose two collar-patch stars can just be seen, wearing German MP40 equipment and marching boots; and at right is an officer cadet, in well-cut breeches and boots. (S. Zaloga)

Regts.; 1,5,51 Art., 51 AT, 1 Recce, 1 Eng. Bns.)

2 Armd. Div. (3 Armd., 3 Mot. Inf. Regts.; 2,6,52 Art., 2 Recce, 2 Eng. Bns.)

1 Cav. (2,3,4 Cav. Regts.; 1 Armd., 1,3,55 Art., 1 Recce, 4 Eng. Bns.)

2nd Cps.—6 Mxd. (3,16,22 Inf. Regts.; 4,5,6,72 Art., 6 Recce, 52 Eng. Bns.)

5 Res. (33,46,52 Inf. Regts.; 34,35,82 Art., 5 Recce, 72 Eng. Bns.)

3rd Cps.—7 Mxd. (4,5,17 Inf. Regts.; 7,8,9,73 Art., 7 Recce, 53 Eng. Bns.)

9 Res. (34,35,47 Inf. Regts.; 37,38,83 Art., 9 Recce, 73 Eng. Bns.)

4th Cps.—10 Mxd. (6,8,18 Inf. Regts.; 10,11,12, 74 Art., 10 Recce, 50 Eng. Bns.)

12 Res. (36,38,48 Inf. Regts.; 40,41,84 Art., 12 Recce, 74 Eng. Bns.)

5th Cps.—13 Mxd. (7,9,20 Inf. Regts.; 13,14,15, 75 Art., 13 Recce, 55 Eng. Bns.)

15 Res. (37, 39, 50 Inf. Regts.; 43,44, 85 Art., 15 Recce, 75 Eng. Bns.)

6th Cps.—16 Mxd. (10,11,19 Inf. Regts.; 16,17, 18,76 Art., 16 Recce, 56 Eng. Bns.)

18 Res. (40,41,49 Inf. Regts.; 46,47,86 Art., 18 Recce, 76 Eng. Bns.)

7th Cps.—20 Mxd. (13,14,23 Inf. Regts.; 19,20, 21,77 Art., 20 Recce, 57 Eng. Bns.)

19 Res. (43,44,53 Inf. Regts.; 49,50,87 Art., 19 Recce, 77 Eng. Bns.)

8th Cps.—24 Mxd. (12,21,24 Inf. Regts.; 22,23, 24,78 Art., 24 Recce, 58 Eng. Bns.)

23 Res. (42,51,54 Inf. Regts.; 52,53,88 Art., 23 Recce, 78 Eng. Bns.)

9th Cps.—25 Mxd. (2,25,26 Inf. Regts.; 2,25,26, 79 Art., 25 Recce, 59 Eng. Bns.)

26 Res. (31,55,56 Inf. Regts.; 55,56,89

Art., 26 Recce, 79 Eng. Bns.)
27 Light (27,57 Inf., 27 Art. Regts.;
27 Recce, 27 Eng. Bns.)

Although 27th Light Div.'s organisation remained unchanged, a Border Guard Group functioned as its third regiment during the 1944 fighting. The Mountain and Frontier Bdes. also remained unchanged, but they were augmented in Transylvania by twenty-seven Szekler Militia battalions. Shortages of equipment seriously delayed this re-organisation, but the eight Mixed Divs. were ready by late 1943 and the Reserve Divs. by spring 1944. Most of these were concentrated in the 'Dead Army', which the Germans refused to release, and which was now made up of the 2nd Reserve Corps (ex-8th Corps, with the 5th, 9th, 12th and 23rd Reserve Divs.) and the

7th Corps (18th and 19th Reserve Divs.).

The armoured divisions were organised along German lines, but the tank battalions had a mixture of Hungarian-made Turan I and II medium tanks. In addition, eight assault artillery battalions were raised. They were to have been equipped with the new Zrinyi assault guns, but in practice there were only enough of these to equip two battalions, and the others which saw action used German StuG IIIs. Originally numbered 1 to 8, the battalions later took the numbers of the Mixed Divs. to which they were supposed to be attached.

Notwithstanding these preparations, Hitler knew that Horthy was secretly trying to find a way out of the war. In March and April 1944 German forces moved into Hungary to ensure her continued adherence to the alliance. The Hungarian army, which had been ordered not to resist, was now fully mobilised for the first time. In May the powerful 1st Army (2nd Armd., 7th, 16th, 20th,

Hungarian officers confer with a German, 1944. Note the field collar patches. Only the officer in the left background wears the regulation flash on the left side of the cap. (K. Barbarski)

24th and 25th Mixed and 27th Light Divs., 1st and 2nd Mountain Bdes.) was sent into Galicia, absorbing the 'Dead Army's' 7th Corps which was already fighting there. By August it had been joined by the remaining first-line divisions (the 6th, 10th and 13th Mixed), but was nevertheless forced to retreat to the Hunyadi Line on the northern Carpathian frontier, where it was able to dig itself in. Meanwhile the élite 1st Cav. Div. had joined the 2nd Reserve Corps in the Pripet area. It distinguished itself in a fighting retreat towards Warsaw and was honoured with the title '1st Hussar Division', after which the whole Corps was repatriated.

Rumania's defection to the Soviet side in August 1944 exposed Hungary's southern frontier. In order to create new formations, the training depots of the Infantry Corps, the Armoured and Cavalry Divisions and the Mountain Brigades were formed into Depot or Szittya ('Scythian') Divisions. Despite the title 'division' they usually had no more than a couple of battalions and artillery batteries each. These, with some units transferred from 1st Army, became the 2nd Army (2nd Armd., 25th Mixed, 27th Light, 2nd, 3rd, 6th, 7th and 9th Depot Divs.; 1st and 2nd Mountain Bdes. and Szekler Militia units), which promptly advanced into eastern Transylvania. Meanwhile, a new but weak 3rd Army (1st Armd., Cavalry Depot, 20th Mixed, 23rd Reserve, 4th, 5th and 8th Depot Divs.) moved into western Transylvania. They were too late to stop the Rumanian and Soviet forces from pouring through the southern Carpathian passes, but they did manage to form a defensive line along the Hungarian-Rumanian frontier. At Arad the 7th Assault Artillery Bn. destroyed 67 Soviet T-34 tanks. Meanwhile, further north, Hungarians who had joined the Soviet forces were trying to persuade Gen. Miklos, commanding 1st Army, to change sides. Miklos, though sympathetic, eventually decided to retreat westwards, followed by the now dangerously exposed 2nd Army.

On 15 October 1944 Horthy, who had continued his secret negotiations with the Allies, proclaimed an armistice. The Germans immediately arrested him and installed the ultra-nationalistic 'Arrow Cross' regime under Szalasi, who was pledged to continue the war. The army now came increasingly under German control. The Corps organisation was broken up, and the three armies were stiffened with German units. Even so, Hitler was by now thoroughly disillusioned with the Hungarian army. In an effort to create a more reliable force the Germans agreed to raise four Hungarian Waffen-SS divisions (25th 'Hunyadi', 26th 'Gombös' and two others) of which none seem to have reached more than regimental strength; and to equip four new Hungarian divisions (to be called 'Kossuth', 'Görgey', 'Petöfi' and 'Klapka'), of which only 'Kossuth' appears to have been formed. The most effective new formation, however, was the élite 'Szent Laszlo' Parachute Division, based on the Parachute Battalion. Orders of Battle were:

'Kossuth'—101, 102, 103 Inf. 101 Art. Regts.
'Szent Laszlo'—1 Para. Bn., 1,2 Elite Inf. Tng. Regts., 1,2 Armd. Tng. Regts., 1,2 Recce Tng. Bns., two river defence Bns., AA Bn.

By Christmas 1944 the 1st Army had retreated into Slovakia and the 2nd Army had been disbanded, transferring its remaining units to the 3rd Army, now south of Lake Balaton, or to the German 6th and 8th Armies in Northern Hungary. Budapest was cut off, defended by a mixed German-Hungarian garrison which included the 1st Armd., 10th Mixed and 12th Reserve Divs.; the Billnitzer Assault Artillery Group (1st Armd. Car and 6th, 8th, 9th and 10th Assault Artillery Bns.); anti-aircraft units, and Szalasi irregular forces. After two unsuccessful German attempts to raise the seige, Budapest surrendered in February 1943. Meanwhile the exhausted 1st Army retreated into Moravia, where it built fortifications until the end of the war. After the failure of the German counter-offensive at Lake Balaton in March the skeletal 3rd Army headed westwards, losing the 1st Hussar Div. near Budapest. Its 2nd Armd., 27th Light, 9th and 23rd Reserve, and 7th and 8th Depot Divs. surrendered to American forces in northern Austria, while the remainder, which included 'Szent Laszlo', fought on the Austro-Yugoslav border before surrendering to the British in May 1945.

In December 1944 the Russians set up a rival Hungarian government under Gen. Miklos, who had finally gone over after the October coup. Hungarian volunteers formed companies and later battalions within Soviet divisions, and a 2,500-strong 'Buda Hungarian Volunteer Regiment' with artillery and tanks. The new government promised to put an army of eight divisions into the field on the Soviet side, but in fact only one division was actually sent to the front, and that arrived too late to see action.

Rumania

1940 was a disastrous year for Rumania. The collapse of her ally France was followed by the Soviet occupation of Bessarabia and Bukovina, then by the loss of half Transylvania to Hungary and the southern Dobrudja to Bulgaria. King Carol had to abdicate in favour of his son Michael, and Gen. Ion Antonescu, a strong-minded soldier, became 'Conducator' or Leader. Antonescu was convinced that Rumania could only regain her lost territories by allying herself with Germany. He signed the Tripartite Pact and asked for German troops to be stationed in Rumania to guarantee her neutrality. The Germans, aware of the importance of Rumania's oil, proceeded to support Antonescu even against an attempted coup by Rumania's own Fascist Party, the Iron Guard. Antonescu was to be a loyal, if not uncritical, ally for the next three years, and was to provide more troops, with fewer reservations regarding their use, than any other satellite leader.

The Rumanian army was not only the largest of the satellite forces but also the one with the longest continuous history. Its performance during the First World War had not been particularly impressive, but a modernisation programme undertaken by King Carol during the 1930s had improved both its equipment and its morale. The war with Russia was by no means unpopular at first, and even after Stalingrad a joint German-Rumanian commission of enquiry found no evidence of defeatism. By 1944 it was a different matter, but by then the Rumanians could see that Germany was beaten. For most of the war they showed themselves to be as the German admitted, 'modest in their needs, resourceful, and capable of tough fighting'.

The pre-war ties between Rumania and France were reflected in the army's organisation and training. Most of the senior officers spoke French rather than German as a second language. France's defeat demonstrated the superiority of German methods, however, and Antonescu lost no time in asking for a German training mission. This began work in October 1940. Training was combat-orientated, concentrating particularly on anti-tank measures and small unit leadership. It was welcomed by the infantry and armoured arms, but there was opposition from some senior officers, and also by the artillery, who considered their own French-inspired techniques to be superior.

In 1939 there had been one Guard and 21 infantry divisions, but three of the latter (12th, 16th and 17th) had to be disbanded after the

July 1941: Gen. Antonescu samples field rations in Bessarabia. His aide is a cavalry officer. Note the cook's distinctive field cap and shirt sleeve order. (Signal)

territorial losses of 1940. Apart from some six security divisions only one other infantry division was raised during the war. This was the 24th, said to have been composed of convicts and Iron Guard political prisoners, and later amalgamated with the 4th Mountain Division. All these divisions were 'triangular', with three infantry and two artillery regiments, signals and engineer battalions, a reconnaissance squadron and anti-tank and machine gun companies. They were numerically strong (17,500 at war establishment) but their artillery was light (52 guns, a mixture of 75mm field guns and 100mm howitzers) and their anti-tank provision inadequate (each regiment had six 37mm guns and the divisional AT company twelve 47mms), which limited their effectiveness, especially in a static defensive rôle. The infantry regiments had a cavalry troop, a support company with mortars and anti-tank guns, and three battalions, each of one machine gun and three rifle companies. The regular

regiments were numbered 1 to 33 and 81 to 96, the first and older group bearing the traditional title 'Dorobanti'. Some divisions contained 'Vanatori' or Rifle regiments, numbered 1 to 10 in a separate series but otherwise identical in organisation.

The élite Mountain Rifles had been formed after the First World War along the lines of the Chasseurs Alpins. Each of the four brigades had one artillery and two rifle regiments, plus a reconnaissance squadron. The basic unit was the battalion. These brigades were renamed 'divisions' in spring 1942, but their organisation remained unchanged. They were smaller than the infantry divisions (about 12,000 men), with much lighter artillery (24 75mm and 100mm mountain guns together with twelve 37mm anti-tank guns). A similar brigade, later 'division', was formed from the élite Frontier Guards.

July 1941: young King Mihai (Michael) in a peaked cap with General (later Marshal) Antonescu in a field cap. (Signal)

Rumanian infantry in the battle for Sebastopol, June 1942. Three wear the M1939 'Dutch' helmet, but the man on the left wears the older French 'Adrian' model. (Signal)

The cavalry were particularly strong. Apart from the Horse Guards there were 25 line cavalry regiments, divided into 'Rosiori' and 'Calarasi', the latter a kind of Yeomanry recruited from prosperous landowners who provided their own horses. Seven Calarasi regiments provided the corps and divisional reconnaissance squadrons, and the remainder were organized into six cavalry brigades (1st, 5th, 6th, 7th, 8th and 9th) with one horse artillery and three cavalry regiments each. A start had been made with mechanisation, three brigades having one mechanised regiment each. The cavalry brigades also became 'divisions' in 1942. Their organisation remained unaltered at the time, though the 7th was later broken up to turn 1st and 8th into four-regiment formations, the latter along Panzer Division lines. These cavalry divisions did well in Russia. Their mobility helped to make up for their numerical weakness (around 6,000 men) and ultra-light artillery (16 75mm field and nine 37mm anti-tank guns), and more than one report speaks of their superior discipline and cohesion compared with the ordinary infantry divisions.

The modernisation programme of the 1930s was only partly successful. The Czech 7.92mm rifle replaced the old 6.5mm Mannlicher and the Czech ZB30 (parent of the famous Bren) was adopted as the squad light machine gun, but many older weapons remained in use. The anti-tank armoury remained weak, though the Germans supplied various captured 47mm guns. Only the Mountain Corps received modern Skoda artillery, and most of the field guns were of First World War vintage, supplemented by booty French and Polish 75mms. Most artillery was horse drawn.

The single tank regiment in existence in 1939 was combined with a motorised rifle regiment in 1941 to form an armoured brigade. This was expanded along German lines in 1942 to form the 1st Armoured Division, later retitled 'Greater Rumania'. Equipment shortages prevented the completion of any other armoured formations, though 5th and 8th Cav. Divs. were in the process of conversion at the time of the Rumanian defection in 1944. The main tank in use at the start of the war was the Skoda LTvz 35, with some CKD light tanks for reconnaissance. Most of the Skodas were lost at Stalingrad (a few were later converted to self-propelled guns using captured 76mm guns) and were replaced by ex-German PzKpfw 38(t)s and IVs. The Czech tanks which were the mainstay of the armoured forces were good in their day but obsolete by comparison with the Russian T-34s.

There was a chronic shortage of motor transport (that allocated to the Don front had a carrying capacity of only 60 tons) and the Germans found themselves forced to help, which caused considerable friction. Inadequate transportation led to the Rumanian depots and hospitals being located too close to the front line, which restricted their freedom of manoeuvre.

Apart from these deficiencies, the Rumanian officer corps had certain weaknesses. The senior commanders were competent enough, even when allowance is made for the presence of a strong German liaison staff, and the officers were undeniably brave—three generals were killed leading bayonet charges at Stalingrad; but the Germans found them as a whole to be unpunctual, negligent and not infrequently corrupt. They showed little regard for the welfare of their men, and maintained rigid social barriers. Nothing, for instance, could induce a Rumanian officer to follow the example of his German colleague and lie down beside his men to correct their aim.

The Rumanians committed their best units to 'Barbarossa'. Their 3rd Army had the Mountain Corps (1st, 2nd and 4th Mtn. Bdes.) and the Cavalry Corps (the part-motorised 5th, 6th and 8th Cav. Bdes.). The 4th Army included the first three German-trained divisions (5th, 6th and 13th) and other élite formations (the Guards Division and the Frontier and Armoured Brigades). It was heavily reinforced during the siege of Odessa (it eventually included the 1st, 2nd, 3rd, 6th, 7th, 8th, 10th, 11th, 14th, 15th, 18th and 21st Infantry and the 35th Reserve Divs., 1st, 7th and 9th Cav. Bdes. and some German units) but it suffered heavy casualties as a result of its deficiencies in training and equipment, and had to be withdrawn for refitting after the city fell in October 1941.

The 3rd Army formations (plus 1st, 2nd, 10th and 18th Inf. Divs.) remained at the front, though now under German control. The Mountain Corps fought in the Crimea under the German 11th Army, and the Cavalry Corps with 1st Panzer Army. Smaller units, such as a Rumanian Mobile Regt. and a ski detachment, also served with German formations during the winter fighting.

The summer of 1942 saw a build-up of Rumanian forces. The Mountain Corps (then 18th Inf. and 1st Mtn. Divs.) was involved in the assault on Sevastopol. In August a largely Rumanian corps (including 18th and 19th Inf., 8th Cav. and 3rd Mtn. Divs.) fought its way across the Kerch Straits, while the 2nd Mtn. Div., rested since the end of 1941, found itself in the Caucasus with the German 3rd Panzer Corps. Gen. Dumitrescu's 3rd Army re-appeared, and in

Rumanian cavalry on the march in 1941 overtake a civilian bus commandeered to help overcome transport deficiencies. Most wear the lightweight summer version of the tunic. (Signal)

Rumanian troops drag their antiquated vehicles through the Russian mud in a scene typifying the primitive conditions of the Eastern Front. (Signal)

October took over the front north of Stalingrad (with 5th, 6th, 9th, 13th, 14th and 15th Inf., 1st and 7th Cav. and 1st Armd. Div.). In the meantime a Rumanian corps came into the line on the south flank. In November it was joined by another, giving six Rumanian divisions (1st, 2nd, 4th and 18th Inf. and 5th and 8th Cav. Divs.) to the German 4th Panzer Army. Hitler proposed that Gen. Constantinescu's 4th Army should take over most of 4th Panzer Army's formations, and that 3rd and 4th Rumanian Armies, together with the German 6th Army in Stalingrad, should form a new 'Army Group Don' under Marshal Antonescu. The 4th Army HQ came forward and was just taking over when the Russian offensive struck the Rumanian-held flanks.

The Rumanian collapse left two divisions (20th Inf., which had been attached to a German corps, and 1st Cav.) trapped inside Stalingrad, and most of the others shattered. The remnants were put into the hastily organised 'Hoth' and 'Hollidt' Groups (the first with 1st, 2nd, 4th and 18th Inf. and 5th and 8th Cav. Divs.; the second with 7th, 9th, 11th and 14th Inf., 7th Cav. and 1st Armd. Divs.); but they had been badly shaken, and by February 1943 they had all been withdrawn for refitting.

This left a number of Rumanian divisions in the Kuban Bridgehead and the Crimea (10th and 19th Inf., 6th and 9th Cav., 1st, 2nd, 3rd and 4th Mtn. Divs.). German policy was to keep them out of the front line, and they were employed mainly on coastal defence and anti-partisan duties throughout 1943. Their morale deteriorated, and when the Russians assaulted the Crimea in April 1944, 10th Inf. and 6th Cav. Divs., which had fought well earlier, collapsed. Most of the troops were evacuated, but had to return to Rumania for reorganisation.

The rest of the Rumanian army was needed to defend Bessarabia. By May 1944 the 3rd and 4th Armies were back in the line. The Rumanians were now able to insist on parity of command, and Army Group Dumitrescu on the right controlled both the 3rd Army and the German 6th Army (its Rumanian formations were 2nd, 14th and 21st Inf., 4th Mtn. and 1st Cav. Divs.). The 4th Army formed part of Army Group Wöhler on the left along with the German 8th Army (the Rumanian formations were the Guards, 1st, 3rd, 4th, 5th, 6th, 11th, 13th and 20th Inf., 5th Cav. and 1st Armd. Divs.). By now, however, the Rumanians had little enthusiasm left for the war; and when the Russians opened their August offensive, concentrating once again on the Rumanians, the front simply collapsed.

King Michael had Antonescu arrested (he was later tried and executed) and Rumania joined the Allies. Her share in the war was by no means over, however, for after some hesitation the Russians decided to use Rumanian formations at the front. A 1st Army (based on the ex-Crimea divisions plus training formations) and a new 4th Army

1: Lance-Corporal, Finnish Infantry, 1944
2: Sergeant, Finnish Artillery, 1942
3: Colonel, Finnish General Staff, 1939

A

1: Private, Hungarian Infantry, 1942
2: Major, Hungarian Cavalry, 1941
3: Major-General, Hungary, 1942

B

1: Private, Rumanian Infantry, 1942
2: Corporal, Rumanian Cavalry, 1942
3: Captain, Rumanian Infantry, 1941

C

1: Trooper, Slovak Cavalry, 1941
2: Lieutenant-Colonel, Slovak General Staff, 1941
3: Lance-Sergeant, Slovak 1st Inf. Div., 1943

D

1: Ski-Trooper, Finnish Frontier Guard, 1940
2: Lance-Corporal, Hungarian Cycle Troops, 1941
3: Major, Italian 'Savoia' Cavalry Regt., 1942

E

1: Sergeant, Hungarian Armoured Troops, 1942
2: Officer tank commander, Finnish Armoured Troops, 1941
3: Lance-Corporal, Rumanian Armoured Troops, 1942

F

1: Warrant Officer Class 2, Hungarian Frontier Guards, 1941
2: Lieutenant, Rumanian Mountain Rifles, 1942
3: Private, Italian 9th Alpini, 1942

G

1: Lance-Sergeant, Parachute Bn., Hungarian 'Szent Laszlo' Div., 1945
2: Major, Rumanian Guards Cavalry Regt., 1941
3: Lance-Corporal, Italian MVSN ('Blackshirts'), 1942

(almost entirely composed of training units) proceeded to fight a bitter campaign in Transylvania. The Rumanians had lost 350,000 men fighting against the Russians and were to lose a further 170,000 against the Germans and Hungarians during this final phase.

Some Rumanians were already fighting with the Russians. The 'Tudor Vladimirescu' Division was formed from prisoners of war in October 1943 and fought in Bessarabia before going on to distinguish itself in Transylvania with the Russian forces. By contrast, a few Rumanians stayed loyal to the Iron Guard government in exile, and two Rumanian regiments were formed by the Waffen-SS.

The composition of the Rumanian divisions was as follows:

Guards—Gd. Regt. 'Mihai Viteazul', 1,2 Gd. Rfl., Gd. Art. Regts., Royal Horse Gds. Sqn.

1st Inf.—85,93 Inf., 5 Rfl., 1,3 Art. Regts., Sqn. 10 Cal.

2nd Inf.—1,26,31 Inf., 9,14 Art. Regts., Sqn. 1 Cal.

3rd Inf.—4,30 Inf., 1 Rfl., 6,15 Art. Regts., Sqn. 1 Cal.

4th Inf.—5,20,21 Inf., 2,10 Art. Regts., Sqn. 4 Cal.

5th Inf.—8,9,32 Inf., 7,28 Art. Regts., Sqn. 6 Cal.

6th Inf.—10,15,27 Inf., 11,16 Art. Regts., Sqn. 6 Cal.

7th Inf.—14,16,37 Inf., 4,8 Art. Regts., Sqn. 12 Cal.

8th Inf.—29 Inf., 7,8 Rfl., 12,17 Art. Regts., Sqn. 12 Cal.

9th Inf.—34,36,40 Inf., 13,18 Art. Regts., Sqn. 4 Cal.

10th Inf.—23,33,38 Inf., 3,20 Art. Regts., Sqn. 4 Cal.

11th Inf.—2,3,19 Inf., 21,26 Art. Regts., Sqn. 1 Cal.

13th Inf.—7,22,89 Inf., 19,41 Art. Regts., Sqn. 6 Cal.

14th Inf.—13,39 Inf., 6 Rfl., 24,29 Art. Regts., Sqn. 12 Cal.

15th Inf.—25,35 Inf., 10 Rfl., 23,25 Art. Regts., Sqn. 8 Cal.

18th Inf.—18,90,92 Inf., 35,36 Art. Regts., Sqn. 10 Cal.

19th Inf.—94,95,96 Inf., 37, 42 Art. Regts., Sqn. 10 Cal.

20th Inf.—82,83,91 Inf., 39,40 Art. Regts., Sqn. 7 Cal.

21st Inf.—11,12,24 Inf., 5,30 Art. Regts., Sqn. 8 Cal.

1st Mtn.—1,2 Mtn. Rfl., 1 Mtn. Art. Regts., Sqn. Mtd. Rfls.

2nd Mtn.—4,5 Mtn. Rfl., 2 Mtn. Art. Regts., Sqn. Mtd. Rfls.

3rd Mtn.—3,6 Mtn. Rfl., 3 Mtn. Art. Regts., Sqn. Mtd. Rfls.

4th Mtn.—8,9 Mtn. Rfl., 4 Mtn. Art. Regts., Sqn. Mtd. Rfls.

Frontier—1,5 F'tier Gd., F'tier Gd. Art. Regts., Sqn. 4 Cal.

1st Cav.—1,2 Ros., 13 Cal., 1 Horse Art. Regts. In 1944 1,2,5 Ros., 11 (Mot.) Cal., 1 Horse Art.

5th Cav.—6 (Mot.), 7,8 Ros., 2 Horse Art. Regts.

6th Cav.—9,10 (Mot.) Ros., 5 Cal., 4 Horse Art. Regts.

7th Cav.—11 (Mot.), 12 Ros., 9 Cal., 5 Horse Art. Regts.

8th Cav.—4 Ros., 2,3 (Mot.) Cal., 3 Horse Art. Regts. In 1944 4 (Armd.) Ros., 3 (Mot. Inf.) Cal., 12 (Mot. Inf.) Ros., 2 (Reece) Cal.

9th Cav.—3,5 Ros., 11 (later 13) Cal., 6 Horse Art. Regts.

1st Armd.—1 Tank, 3,4 Mot. Rfl., 1 Mot. Art. Regts.

Slovakia

In 1939 Hitler took advantage of the existence of a strong Slovak separatist movement to destroy Czechoslovakia. He forced the Slovaks to declare their independence by threatening that unless they did he would hand them over to the Hungarians, to whom they had belonged before 1918. The new state had no option but to accept German protection and become a model satellite. The Premier, Monsignor Jozef Tiso, set up a one party state with a party militia, the Hlinka Guards, modelled on the Storm Troopers.

Slovakia was allowed to maintain its own army, and inherited the Czechoslovakian equipment stored within its borders. Since the Slovak officers were all ex-Czechoslovakian army too, the new force bore a strong resemblance to that highly fact the first of the satellites to join what Tiso called the 'crusade against Bolshevism'.

In the early days of 'Barbarossa', Army Group South included a Slovak Army Corps of two divisions (1st and 2nd), but these lacked mobility and were used mainly for security duties. The most effective Slovak formation was an ad hoc 'Mobile Brigade', consisting of single tank, motorised infantry, artillery and engineer battalions. During August 1941 it was decided to send the infantry divisions back to Slovakia and to form a 10,000-strong Mobile Division and a 6,000-strong Security Division. These were placed under German operational control, though the administration remained wholly Slovak. In 1942 the Slovaks suggested sending a third division to form a Slovak Corps, but this offer was not accepted.

The élite Mobile Division fought at Lemberg, at Kiev and on the Mius during the winter of 1941–42, where one German officer found the men to be 'brave soldiers with very good discipline'. It

Lt. Gen. Ferdinand Čatloš, the Slovak Minister of Defence, between two German officers. Note the khaki velvet collar of his officer's greatcoat. (Heeresgeschichtliches Museum, Vienna)

professional body, though the units had to be re-organised from scratch. One unusual feature was that the Volksdeutsche served in their own 'closed' formations, which at one point amounted to one artillery, one engineer and two infantry regiments.

The Slovak army had three infantry divisions by the time war broke out. It helped the Germans in their attack on Poland, and two divisions (the 1st and 3rd) occupied territory which the Slovaks claimed was theirs. This co-operation did much to establish Slovakia's status as a loyal German ally and to avert the threat of a Hungarian take-over. Nevertheless, the Slovaks thought it prudent to offer to help the Germans against the Russians providing that the Hungarians did, and were in

Maj. Gen. Agust Malár, commander of the Slovak Mobile Division from December 1941 to July 1942, one of the two Slovak officers to be awarded the German Knight's Cross. (Friedrich Herrmann)

A Slovak infantryman presents arms. Note the double chin strap of the Czech M1934 helmet and the unit badge at the side of the collar. (Heeresgeschichtliches Museum, Vienna)

took part in the capture of Rostov alongside SS-Div. 'Wiking', then advanced into the Kuban with 1st Panzer Army. It helped to cover the retreat from the Caucasus after Stalingrad, and was nearly cut off near Krasnodar before the survivors were airlifted to the Crimea, leaving their heavy equipment behind. Meanwhile, the Security Division was serving in the Ukraine.

During 1943 the Mobile Division was re-organised as the 1st Infantry Division and was relegated to coastal defence duties. Morale slumped, and both divisions began to lose men through desertion. The Slovaks suggested trans-ferring them to the Balkans or Western Europe, but the Germans refused. They then asked for their recall to Slovakia, but the Germans refused again, though they did agree not to use them in the line without Slovak approval. When a Russian breakthrough forced them to break this promise the troops proved to be unreliable. In 1944 they were put into reserve, disarmed and converted into Construction Brigades, the 1st serving in Rumania and Hungary and the 2nd in Italy.

Meanwhile, the Slovaks had organised two new divisions (1st and 2nd Infantry) to defend the Carpathians. A third was forming in central Slovakia when the Partisan movement initiated a rising in late August 1944. This was premature from the army's point of view, and the Germans were able to disarm the two field divisions. Many soldiers joined the Partisans in central Slovakia and held out until the end of October, helped by an Allied Czechoslovakian Airborne Brigade flown in by the Russians which included many ex-

Ex-Czech LT vz.38 tanks of the Slovak Army with the post-1942 shield markings. The crew wear Czech overalls. (Bundesarchiv, Koblenz)

members of the Mobile Division.

The Tiso government remained in power supported by the armed Hlinka Guard and a small force of loyal troops. In February 1945 these amounted to one infantry regiment, a flak regiment and an artillery battery. All the Volksdeutsche were transferred to the Wehrmacht in exchange for Germans of Slovak origin. Some of the disarmed Slovak troops were formed into two more Construction Brigades.

The Slovak army used mainly Czechoslovakian equipment, though the Germans supplied some mortars and anti-tank, field and AA guns. The Slovak policy was one of rapid rotation between the Home Army and the divisions in Russia, and they even went so far as to discharge conscripts when their period of service was over throughout the war. In general the policy of maintaining one élite formation in the field was successful, at least up to 1943, for the Mobile Division was well thought of by the Germans and was used by them in a front-line rôle.

The Slovakian-based infantry divisions were conventional triangular formations with partly-mounted reconnaissance elements and horse-drawn artillery. The Mobile Division had two small infantry regiments, an artillery regiment with three nine-gun battalions and a reconnaissance battalion, all motorised, plus a tank company with twelve Czech LTvz 35, 38 or 40 tanks. The Security Division also had two regiments with a horse-drawn artillery regiment, a partly motorised reconnaissance battalion, and an armoured car platoon which was later transferred to the Mobile Division. The divisional units were as follows:

Mobile Div. (1st Inf., 1943–44)—20,21 Inf., 11 Art. Regts., 5 Recce Bn., 11 Tank. Coy. (disbanded '43)
Sec'ty Div.—101,102 Inf., 31 Art. Regts., 12 Recce Bn.
1st Inf. Div.—(1941 & 1944)—1,2,3 Inf., 1 Art. Regts., 1 Recce Bn.
2nd Inf. Div.—(1941 & 1944)—4,5,6 Inf., 2 Art. Regts., 2 Recce Bn.

Other Allies

Mussolini was convinced that **Italy** would gain both prestige and booty by joining in the German attack on the Soviet Union, and sent the 60,000-strong 'Italian Expeditionary Corps in Russia' (C.S.I.R.) of three divisions. 'Pasubio' and 'Torino' were 1938-type binary divisions with two infantry regiments and an artillery regiment each, plus other services. The 3rd Mobile Division 'Principe Amedeo Duca d'Aosta' had two mounted cavalry regiments, a Bersaglieri cyclist regiment, a light tank group with obsolete L-3s, an artillery regiment and service units. Later he sent the 63rd Assault Legion 'Tagliamento' to represent the Blackshirts.

In July 1941 the supposedly motorised C.S.I.R. followed the German forces through the Ukraine, mainly on foot. Morale was high at the prospect of an easy campaign, and the Germans were impressed; but this initial euphoria soon disappeared. Inadequate leadership, armour and motorisation, and a shortage of artillery and anti-tank weapons revealed the Corps to be ill-equipped for the fighting it was to encounter.

Undeterred, in March 1942 Mussolini sent the 2nd Corps ('Sforzesca', 'Ravenna' and 'Cosseria' Inf. Divs.) and the élite Alpine Corps ('Vicenza' Infantry and 'Tridentina', 'Julia' and 'Cuneense' Alpine Divs.) plus further Blackshirt units (formed into the '3 Gennaio' and '23 Marzo' Groups) to join the C.S.I.R., now designated 35th Corps.

Gen. Giovanni Messe (2nd right), commander of the Italian CSIR, inspects transport units of the 'Torino' Division, Russia 1941. (Friedrich Herrmann)

A captain of the German Army's Croat Legion. Most Croats wore German uniforms with Croatian field caps and badges, but this officer's tunic may also be Croat Army issue. (Friedrich Herrmann)

Colonel Carlo Pagliano, commander of the 'Novaro' Cavalry regiment in Russia, 1941. Note the white 'flames', the ribbon of the Iron Cross 2nd class, and the War Academy eagle breast badge. (Friedrich Herrmann)

This 227,000-man force became the 8th Army. In August it was guarding the Don front north of Stalingrad, with German liaison officers and formations attached to ensure its reliability. Although a Russian attack had been expected, the Italians were unable to resist the massive armoured thrust of 11 December 1942. The 2nd and 35th Corps crumbled almost immediately, leaving the Alpine Corps stranded and opening up a huge gap in the Don defences. In January 1943 the survivors regrouped in the Ukraine, but the disillusioned Germans sent them back to Italy, where they blamed both Hitler and Mussolini for the sufferings they had endured.

Croatia, which was divided into Italian and German spheres of influence, sent contingents to serve with both the Italian and German armies in Russia. The Italian-Croat Legion was organised as a two-battalion Blackshirt Legion with an artillery battalion attached. It fought well with the Italian 3rd Mobile Div., but was destroyed during the Don retreat. The German-Croat Legion was organised as a three-battalion infantry regiment with an attached artillery battalion, and was known as the '369th Reinforced Croat Infantry Regiment'. It was lost at Stalingrad. Some of the captured Croats later fought with the Red Army as part of the '1st Royal Yugoslav Brigade In The Soviet Union'.

Contingents from other European states fought in Russia wearing German Army uniform with national armshields. The 250th Infantry 'Blue Division', composed of Spanish volunteers, fought until October 1943 in Northern Russia[1]. The French Volunteer Legion (L.V.F.) fought until September 1944 as the '638th Reinforced Infantry Regiment', whilst Belgian volunteers served in the 'Walloon Infantry Battalion No. 373' in Southern

[1] See MAA 103, *Germany's Spanish Volunteers 1941–45*

Russia until August 1943. These troops usually acquitted themselves well, often suffering heavy losses, and many subsequently transferred to the Waffen-SS.

The Plates

A1: Korporaali (Lance-Corporal), Finnish Infantry, July 1944

This soldier wears the short, typically shabby light grey summer tunic which seems to have replaced the earlier grey shirt-blouse almost completely, possibly because of the latter's Russian appearance. Due to material shortages he has no identifying collar patches and wears his gold rank chevron on his shoulder straps. On his right sleeve is the newly introduced tank-destroyer badge, clearly modelled on the German version, and awarded by divisional commanders on the recommendation of company commanders for the single-handed destruction of three enemy tanks. If five tanks were destroyed a narrow white bar was added above, with an extra bar for every additional five tanks. He wears the M1935 German helmet which had largely replaced the M1918, but Finnish troops also wore Czech, Hungarian, Italian and Swedish helmets. He carries the Suomi submachine gun and one of the German Panzerfaust anti-tank projectiles hurriedly supplied to counter the Soviet threat.

A2: Kersantti (Sergeant), Finnish Artillery, 1942

This Sergeant, probably a senior battery NCO in charge of a field gun, is on stand-to behind the front line. His unpretentious but soldierly appearance typifies the uncomplicated and determined philosophy of the Finnish Army. He wears the 1936 winter field uniform which remained unchanged until well after 1945. It was standardised throughout the Army and Air Force, so that his branch is discernible only by the red and black of the collar patches and by the branch badge on the shoulder straps. As a regular NCO he wears gold chevrons on the collar patches. Later the gold was sometimes replaced by yellow, whilst conscripts and reservists, owing to material shortages, wore blank collar patches or omitted them altogether, and white transverse bars on the shoulder straps

as rank insignia. He wears the breeches and field boots of a pre-war regular: lower ranks wore trousers tucked into marching boots. His uniform is markedly German in appearance, only the Finnish insignia and the absence of a greenish tone to the grey cloth distinguishing him from a German soldier.

A3: Eversti (Colonel), Finnish General Staff, 1939

The uniforms in which Finland fought the Second World War were introduced in 1936. They preserved a markedly German appearance, reflecting the aid given to the fledgling Finnish Republic by Germany in 1918, and the high reputation the German military enjoyed in Finland between the wars. This officer, probably the chief-of-staff of an infantry division, wears the undress uniform which in wartime tended to be restricted to generals and senior officers. The distinctive fly-fronted tunic carries the same insignia as the field uniform: branch-coloured collar patches showing rank, and on the shoulder straps the brass Finnish lion worn by all officers, usually with a brass branch badge above it (the General Staff did not wear this). At his throat he wears the 'Mannerheim Cross of the Cross of Liberty', awarded for gallantry in battle. The colourful breeches and German-style peaked cap were progressively replaced after 1939 by plain breeches in the uniform colour and the peaked field cap.

B1: Honvéd (Private), Hungarian Infantry, summer 1942

The pre-war Hungarian summer uniform consisted of a light khaki fly-fronted tunic. However, the shirt sleeve order illustrated here seems to have been introduced in 1941 and was commonly worn during the Russian summer. The shirt, with its collar, breast pockets and tunic-front is very advanced for the period, as is the fact that the trousers can be worn without braces. The Hungarians saw themselves as the standard bearers of European civilization in Eastern Europe, and condemned the Soviet practice of wearing the shirt outside the trousers as Slav barbarism. The trouser-breeches and leather anklets are traditionally Hungarian. This member of the ill-fated 2nd Army wears no identifying insignia in this

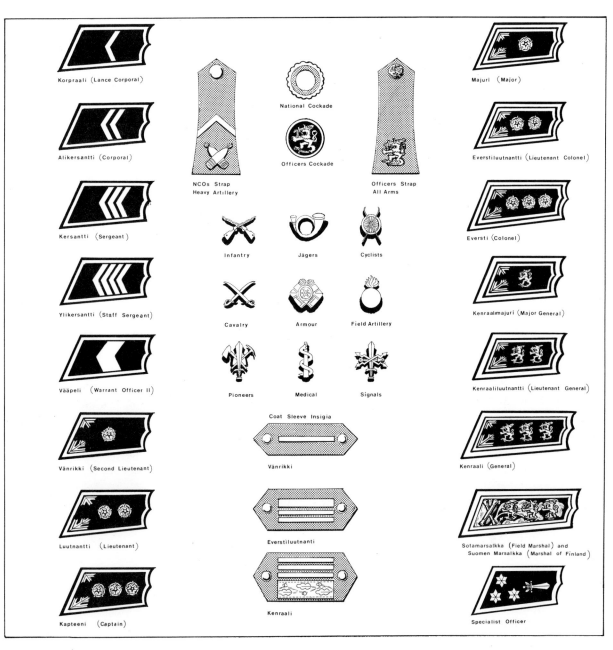

Korpraali (Lance Corporal)

Alikersantti (Corporal)

Kersantti (Sergeant)

Ylikersantti (Staff Sergeant)

Vääpeli (Warrant Officer II)

Vänrikki (Second Lieutenant)

Luutnantti (Lieutenant)

Kapteeni (Captain)

NCOs Strap Heavy Artillery

National Cockade

Officers Cockade

Officers Strap All Arms

Infantry

Jägers

Cyclists

Cavalry

Armour

Field Artillery

Pioneers

Medical

Signals

Coat Sleeve Insigia

Vänrikki

Everstiluutnanti

Kenraali

Majuri (Major)

Everstiluutnantti (Lieutenant Colonel)

Eversti (Colonel)

Kenraalimajuri (Major General)

Kenraaliluutnantti (Lieutenant General)

Kenraali (General)

Sotamarsalkka (Field Marshal) and
Suomen Marsalkka (Marshal of Finland)

Specialist Officer

order of dress, and carries the standard 8mm Steyr Stutze rifle. He wears the M1938 helmet, which was almost identical to the German M1935 except that it had a rectangular bracket at the back, allowing it to be hung from the belt whilst on the march.

B2: Örnagy (Major), Hungarian Cavalry, July 1941
This officer, probably the commander of a mounted squadron, wears the officer's field dress, which is identical with the service dress except that the light blue cavalry collar patches omit the

FINLAND. The national cockade was white and light blue. The officers' lion cockade was gold on red: NCOs wore a similar cockade all in silver. Branch devices, marshal's oak leaf embroidery, officers' rosettes, lions and sleeve braids were gold. Greatcoat sleeve braids were light grey. NCO's chevrons were gold, but conscript NCOs often wore white bars. Patches were of branch colour with a contrasting colour frame as follows: Infantry—dark green/grey; Jägers —dark green/yellow; Cavalry—yellow/grey; Armour— yellow/grey; Artillery—red/black; Engineers—purple/grey; Medical—magenta/grey; General Staff—crimson/grey; Frontier Guards—dark green/orange; Guards—blue/white.

outside braiding. The field cap was inherited from the Austro-Hungarian cavalry, but in the Hungarian Army it was worn by all branches. It carries rank insignia of gold braid in the same sequence as on the greatcoat cuff, but in the form of chevrons, with the thicker braids above the thinner. The cap flash is in the branch colour, which was light blue for cavalry until 1 October 1942, when it became the dark blue of the new 'Mobile Troops'. The tunic is the standard pattern, with gold buttons for officers. Thin gold shoulder cords with red interwoven threads are worn on both shoulders, another Austro-Hungarian tradition. Before the war branches other than cavalry, artillery and horse transport only wore these on the right shoulder. Unusually, this officer is still wearing the leather crossbelt which, following German practice, was not normally worn in wartime.

B3: Vezérőrnagy (Major-General), Hungary, parade uniform, 1942

The Hungarians considered themselves to be the successors of the old Austro-Hungarian Empire, and modelled their parade uniform for Army officers after that of the Imperial Army. By 1942 the earlier hussar-style tunic had been replaced by the version shown here, but the matt-black kepi copies the Imperial model except for the Hungarian national cockade on the front. The trousers, identical to the Imperial 'Salonhosen', were black with narrow red piping for all ranks except Generals, who had two thick stripes. All braiding and metal fittings were in gold for officers. General officers of infantry, artillery, general staff, mobile or technical troops wore red collar patches, while other generals used the appropriate branch colour. Regular NCOs wore a similar uniform, but the kepi and trousers were khaki and the braiding and fittings silver. This officer wears the Iron Cross 2nd Class alongside his Hungarian decorations, which follow Imperial practice in having triangular ribbons.

C1: Soldat (Private), Rumanian Infantry, December 1942

This soldier is one of the survivors of the badly mauled 20th Infantry Division trapped with the German 6th Army in the Stalingrad pocket. The regulation fur hat was made in both black and white lambswool. Later a Russian-style cap was issued. His greatcoat is standard, the only insignia

authorised being rank devices. Officers wore a coat of better quality, and Generals left the top buttons undone to display lapel facings, which were red from 1941. Officers could also wear a leather coat with straight gold rank bars 55mm long in the same sequence as on the field cap. This soldier wears M1930 breeches and puttees, officially replaced after 1939 by trousers and anklets. He wears his ammunition pouches without shoulder braces and carries the obsolete Mannlicher M1893 6.5mm rifle.

C2: Sergent (Corporal), Rumanian Cavalry, 1942

This cavalryman wears the extremely practical field uniform for junior NCOs and men. The tunic, made of coarse khaki material, was introduced in 1939 and, contrary to several post-war reports, never bore collar patches. The only insignia is the single gold braid rank bar on the distinctive rectangular shoulder straps, and indeed only the boots identify this man as a cavalryman—photos show many wearing trousers instead of breeches. The steel helmet was worn in combat, but behind the front lines the field cap, with its traditional Rumanian double-peak design. Long worn by all NCOs and men, it was adopted by officers in 1940 and worn with rank insignia on the front in the form of gold braid chevrons. The belt is standard, but dismounted troops wore trousers, ankle puttees or leather gaiters, and boots. This field tunic was sometimes worn by officers with the appropriate belt and rank insignia. The weapon is the Rumanian M1941 Orita 9mm sub-machine gun, though the Beretta M38A was also used.

C3: Capitán (Captain), Rumanian Infantry, late 1941

In 1930 the Rumanian Army adopted khaki uniforms, and this officer, probably the commander of an infantry company, wears the modified field uniform in use from 1941 to 1947. His helmet is the distinctive Dutch 23/27 model, issued to the Rumanians in 1939 and worn by them alongside the M1915 French 'Adrian' helmet. The front bears the double 'C' and crown monogram of King Carol II, although King Mihai (Michael) had ascended the throne in September 1940. Both plain and 'C' monogram helmets were worn, the former becoming standard in 1942. The tunic dates from 1934, but was

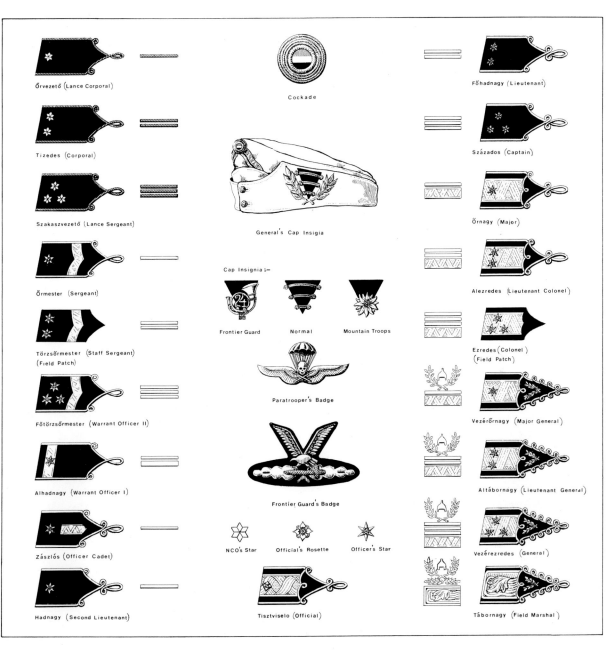

Őrvezető (Lance Corporal)

Tizedes (Corporal)

Szakaszvezető (Lance Sergeant)

Őrmester (Sergeant)

Törzsőrmester (Staff Sergeant) (Field Patch)

Fötörzsőrmester (Warrant Officer II)

Alhadnagy (Warrant Officer I)

Zászlós (Officer Cadet)

Hadnagy (Second Lieutenant)

Cockade

General's Cap Insigia

Cap Insignia :—

Frontier Guard   Normal   Mountain Troops

Paratrooper's Badge

Frontier Guard's Badge

NCO's Star   Official's Rosette   Officer's Star

Tisztviselo (Official)

Főhadnagy (Lieutenant)

Százados (Captain)

Őrnagy (Major)

Alezredes (Lieutenant Colonel)

Ezredes (Colonel) (Field Patch)

Vezérőrnagy (Major General)

Altábornagy (Lieutenant General)

Vezérezredes (General)

Tábornagy (Field Marshal)

modified in 1941 with brown bone or leather buttons, plain khaki shoulder straps and thin gold braid rank bars. The dark blue infantry collar patches adopted in 1941 replaced a complicated system of red, dark red or blue patches commemorating regimental origins. The Captain wears the Iron Cross 1st Class and the Order of 'Mihai Viteazul' (Michael the Brave). A similar uniform in coarser cloth and no cross belt was worn by senior NCOs.

HUNGARY. The cockade was red over white over green. The braid surround, like the cap flash braiding, collar patch edging and sleeve stripes was gold for officers, silver for NCOs and brown for junior NCOs and other ranks. Field collar patches omitted the braid. Junior NCOs wore white stars, senior NCOs silver stars and chevrons ('Alhadnagy' had a gold vertical bar and gold over silver sleeve stripes), company officers gold stars, and other officers silver stars on gold braid. Generals' patches had gold oak leaves. The Frontier Guards' horn was gold, the Mountain Troops' edelweiss silver with a gold centre. The Paratroop wings were bronze: an embroidered version had gold wings with silver skull and daggers. The Frontier Guards' eagle was brown, silver or gold according to rank. Branch colours were: Generals and Artillery—red; General Staff—black velvet, edged red; Infantry (including Lorried, Paratroops, Frontier and Mountain)—grass green; Cavalry (to 1942)— light blue; Mobile Troops—dark blue; Medical Officers— black velvet; Technical Troops—dark green.

D1: Strelník (Trooper), Slovak Cavalry, 1941
This cavalryman wears the winter field uniform which, apart from the insignia, is identical to that of the former Czechoslovakian Army. The standard greatcoat bears yellow cavalry collar patches and has bronze buttons for other ranks. Boots and spurs are the normal cavalry issue, and the ex-Czech equipment includes the M1924 rifle. The helmet, with its distinctive silhouette and double chin strap, was adopted by the Czech Army in 1934. It went on to equip the Slovakian, Bohemia-Moravian and short-lived Ruthenian forces, and was subsequently utilised in limited numbers by the Finns, Yugoslavs, Germans and Italians. For the Russian campaign the Slovaks painted the rim blue and added the Slovak cross on both sides, presumably to avoid confusion with the Soviet helmet.

D2: Podplukovník (Lieutenant-Colonel), Slovak General Staff, 1941
Initially the Slovaks used Czechoslovakian uniforms with new Slovak cap badges. New uniforms and insignia were prescribed in May 1939, and insignia was further altered in late 1940 to the definitive form illustrated. Nevertheless the economic situation caused obsolete uniforms and badges to be worn until the end of the war. This officer's tunic, though open at the collar, is basically Czech, but the collar rank insignia and single shoulder cord reflects Austro-Hungarian (and incidentally German Sturmabteilung) practice, while the cap insignia is clearly modelled on the Wehrmacht's. The principle of gold insignia for officers, silver for NCOs and bronze for other ranks followed Czech and Hungarian practice. His staff officer status is shown by red collar patches, piping and trouser stripes.

D3: Catník (Lance-Sergeant), 1st Slovak Infantry Division, 1943
This NCO, probably a platoon sergeant in the 20th or 21st Infantry Regiment, is behind the lines in the Crimea. He wears the field uniform, also worn by officers, who substituted a Sam Browne belt, gold buttons, a single gold shoulder cord and appropriate insignia. The uniform is basically that of the former Czechoslovakian Army except for the tunic. This never succeeded in entirely replacing the fly-fronted Czech tunic with its patch pockets, though the latter was sometimes modified by the addition of six visible buttons. The rank insignia and buttons are silver for NCOs. The collar patch, maroon for infantry, has a single silver bar at the rear edge indicating two years' service in the army. Following Czech practice a regimental number, in silver for NCOs, is worn behind the collar patch, but is removed when in the field. The breast badge commemorates service in the Mobile Division.

E1: Finnish Frontier Guard Ski-Trooper, 1940
The Frontier Guard units of the Finnish Army have always been regarded as an élite corps, and they particularly impressed the Germans with their ability to operate independently in difficult terrain. In fact virtually all Finns could ski, and this winter mobility was used to devastating effect. Many types of snow camouflage were worn, but this two-piece coverall with elasticated trousers worn under or over the jacket seems to have been the most common. Footwear was even less standardised: this trooper is wearing ski-boots with turned-up toes which probably originated from Finnish Lapland. No insignia is worn on the coverall, and as he has omitted his collar patches his rank cannot be ascertained. His only badge is the standard national cockade on his winter field cap, an early model without the Russian-style earflaps which later became standard. He carries the exceptionally reliable Suomi sub-machine gun.

E2: Örvezetö (Lance-Corporal), Hungarian Cyclists, 1941
Cyclist battalions were needed to make up the numbers in the inadequately motorised 'Mobile Corps', which by 1941 was spearheading the forces re-occupying those territories which Hungary claimed as her own. The greatcoat is standard issue. As a soldier below senior NCO rank he wears bronze buttons and the traditional Austro-Hungarian 'spearhead' collar patch in the branch colour. Senior NCOs added a silver button, officers a gold one and generals had both a gold button and laurel leaf embroidery. Late issue collar patches sometimes had straight sides. Cyclists wore infantry green until 1 October 1942,

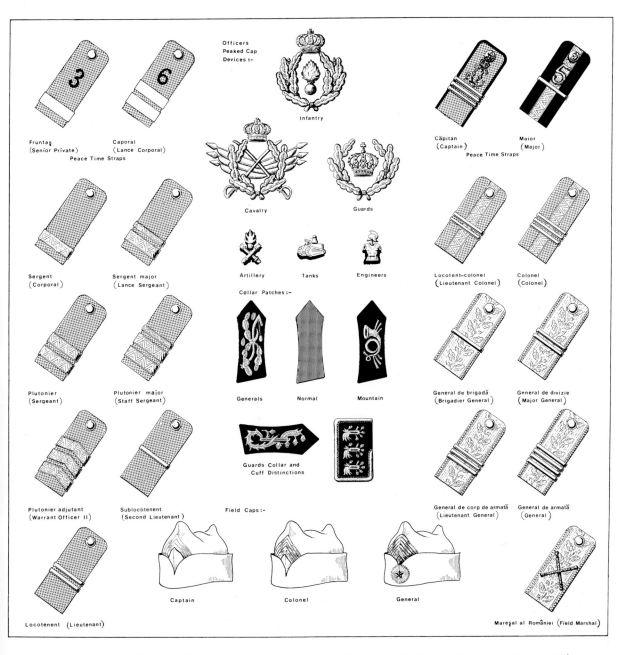

Officers Peaked Cap Devices :-

Infantry

Cavalry

Guards

Fruntaş (Senior Private)

Caporal (Lance Corporal)

Peace Time Straps

Artillery

Tanks

Engineers

Collar Patches :-

Sergent (Corporal)

Sergent major (Lance Sergeant)

Generals

Normal

Mountain

Plutonier (Sergeant)

Plutonier major (Staff Sergeant)

Guards Collar and Cuff Distinctions

Plutonier adjutant (Warrant Officer II)

Sublocotenent (Second Lieutenant)

Field Caps :-

Captain

Colonel

General

Locotenent (Lieutenant)

Căpitan (Captain)

Maior (Major)

Peace Time Straps

Locotent–colonel (Lieutenant Colonel)

Colonel (Colonel)

General de brigadă (Brigadier General)

General de divizie (Major General)

General de corp de armată (Lieutenant General)

General de armată (General)

Mareşal al României (Field Marshal)

thereafter the dark blue of the Mobile Troops. Just visible under the greatcoat is the high collar of the obsolete M1922 tunic. He wears the old M1917 helmet and carries on his back his field pack and rolled blanket. The rifle is the M1895 Mannlicher Repetierstütze, converted to fire the Hungarian 8mm cartridge. Note short brown rank stripes on cuffs.

E3: Maggiore (Major), Italian 'Savoia' Cavalry Regiment, late 1942

By 1941 cavalry were regarded as obsolete, but

RUMANIA. Cap badges and collar patch embroidery were gold for officers and yellow for NCOs, except for the generals' 'sunburst' device which was silver with a gold star. Pre-war shoulder straps had branch-colour number (NCOs and men), piping (company officers) or bases (senior officers), with silver numbers or cyphers for officers. Post-1941 straps had plain khaki grounds. Rank bars were of yellow wool for junior NCOs, of gold braid for senior NCOs and all officers. Field officers and generals had gold centre braids. Cap rank braids were gold. Non-combatant branches wore white or silver insignia. The marshal's batons were silver. The 1941 branch colours were as follows: Generals—red; General Staff—black velvet; Infantry—dark blue; Frontier Guard—light green; Mountain Rifles—green; Cavalry—cherry red; Mechanized Troops—ash grey; Artillery and Engineers—black; Technical Troops—yellow piped red.

they were to prove invaluable for attacking straggling infantry in the trackless wastes of Russia, and 'Savoia' mounted one of the last cavalry charges of all time on 24 August 1942 near Tschebarevskij on the Don. The officer illustrated wears the standard M1934 field uniform in officer's grey with cavalry breeches and boots, the black cross of the Royal House of Savoy on his helmet, and his regiment's red tie. The tunic had been modified in 1940, receiving a plain collar and shoulder straps, and small yellow rayon rank stripes on the cuffs, whilst the breeches lost their coloured piping. The cavalry's three-pointed collar 'flames', black for this unit, carry the star of the Italian Armed Forces; they received red piping in 1942, presumably to commemorate Russian service. The sword is the normal cavalry model, although many cavalrymen adopted the Cossack 'shashka', to which they added the black sword knot.

F1: Örmester (Sergeant), Hungarian Armoured Troops, late 1942

Italian influence on the Hungarian Army was eventually superseded by German, but this NCO still cuts a distinctly Italian figure. His padded black leather AFV helmet is the Italian M1935 model, although field caps and steel helmets were also worn, and a modified leather helmet with earphones and a squarer crown was issued later. His leather jacket also follows Italian patterns, though the pre-war Czech khaki overalls were also worn. The buttons were silver for senior NCOs, and the collar is faced with khaki uniform cloth, but it is not clear whether collar patches were intended to be worn with this jacket. In any case the wide collar exposes part of the collar of the field tunic worn underneath. These field collar patches lacked the silver NCOs' looped braid, and are dark blue for armoured troops. The trousers and footwear are standard infantry issue. The weapon is the Pisztoly 37M.

F2: Finnish Officer Tank Commander, late 1941

After the Winter War the modest Finnish tank force was expanded using captured Soviet armoured vehicles. The four tank companies were re-organised into the 1st, 2nd and 3rd Tank Battalions and the 1st Independent Tank Platoon,

all equipped exclusively with enemy armour. These units advanced with the rest of the army at the beginning of the Continuation War, and were incorporated into the new Armoured Division in August 1943. The commander illustrated reflects this tradition of rugged adaptability. He wears the standard side cap with its distinctive chin strap and the black piping of Armoured Troops. Although he wears the other ranks' blue and white cockade his status as an officer is shown by his belt and cross belt. Over his field tunic he wears a very practical leather jacket. Rank insignia were sometimes worn on this garment, in the form of plain rosettes on the collar for officers and (presumably) chevrons or bars on the shoulder straps for NCOs. Captured Soviet tank helmets were almost universal.

F3: Caporal (Lance-Corporal), Rumanian Armoured Troops, 1942

This tank crewman wears a uniform showing both French and Czech influences. The large black beret pulled down over the right ear is clearly French-inspired, and replaces the peaked or field caps of other branches. Officers wore a better quality version with a silver badge depicting a French Renault tank within a circlet of oak and laurel leaves. In action the French M1923 tank helmet was worn, painted dark blue. The overalls are the distinctive Czech model, buttoning at cuffs and ankles. Hungarian and Slovakian tank crews wore the same overalls, in both cases with the normal field cap, and their ubiquity indicates how advanced the Czechs had been in armoured warfare. The belt is standard army issue, and tank commanders wore a holstered pistol; this NCO has a slung Orita SMG (see C2).

G1: Fötörzörmester (Warrant Officer II), Hungarian Frontier Guards, 1941

Frontier Battalions were ordinary infantry units, originally recruited separately to circumvent the restrictions of the Treaty of Trianon. Many were stationed in occupied northern Transylvania and Ruthenia. This senior NCO wears the standard service dress with Frontier Guard distinctions. The normal field cap had a soft visor which could be unfolded, but Frontier and Mountain Troops' caps had fixed visors. The cap flash is infantry

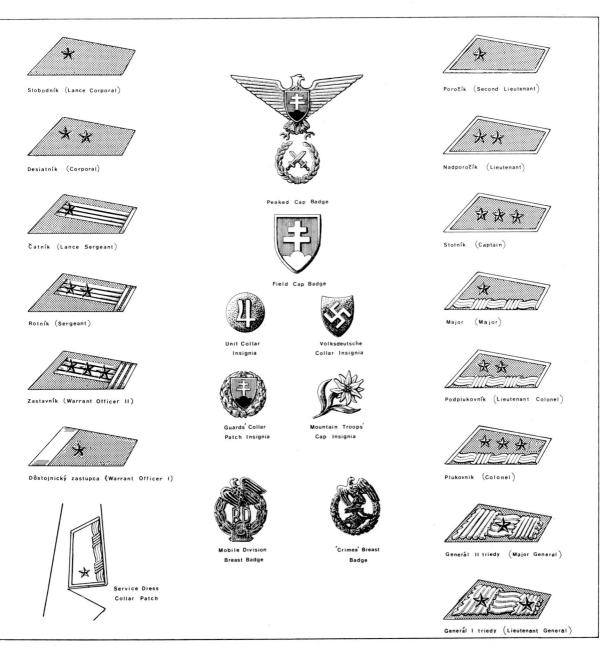

Slobodník (Lance Corporal)

Desiatník (Corporal)

Čatník (Lance Sergeant)

Rotník (Sergeant)

Zastavník (Warrant Officer II)

Dôstojnický zastupca (Warrant Officer I)

Service Dress Collar Patch

Peaked Cap Badge

Field Cap Badge

Unit Collar Insignia

Volksdeutsche Collar Insignia

Guards' Collar Patch Insignia

Mountain Troops' Cap Insignia

Mobile Division Breast Badge

'Crimea' Breast Badge

Poročík (Second Lieutenant)

Nadporočík (Lieutenant)

Stotník (Captain)

Major (Major)

Podplukovník (Lieutenant Colonel)

Plukovník (Colonel)

Generál II triedy (Major General)

Generál I triedy (Lieutenant General)

green, with a green cock's feather and a gold hunting horn bearing the battalion number. The tunic has branch-colour shoulder straps, and silver NCO's buttons, collar patch braid and Frontier Guards' eagle breast badge. In the field khaki shoulder straps and braidless collar patches were worn, and the feather was removed. The silver triangle on the left sleeve, edged with black and the branch colour, identified a regular NCO.

SLOVAKIA. The eagle and crossed swords device was gold with a coloured shield bearing a white Slovak cross over blue mountains on red ground. The field cap badge was supposed to be gold, silver or bronze according to rank. The Guards' collar badge bore the coloured shield. The commemorative breast badges were silver. NCOs' rank stars and vertical braid bars (the lattern denoting length of service) were silver, the horizontal braids silver and red. The 'Dôstojnický zastipan' wore a silver star and gold braid. Officers' braid and stars were gold, except for the generals' stars which were silver. Collar patch branch colours were: Generals, General Staff and Artillery—red; Infantry—maroon; Cavalry —yellow; Armour—pink; Reconnaissance—brown; Engineers and Medical—dark green (Medical Officers with a red vertical bar at the rear); Technical Troops—green; Transport—ochre.

G2: Locotenent (Lieutenant), Rumanian Mountain Rifles, 1942

The Rumanian Mountain Troops were only formed after the First World War, but they rapidly established themselves as an élite corps. Their version of the officers' tunic could be worn with the collar open or closed, but this officer, probably a platoon commander, wears a later pattern which was only worn closed. His collar patches are green for Rifles; Mountain Artillery wore black and Mountain Engineers coffee brown. The distinctive beret, clearly inspired by that of the Chasseurs Alpins, was ash grey for service dress and khaki in the field. The cap badge was a gold hunting horn on a green patch (though at least one officer wore the Edelweiss badge of the German Mountain Troops). Mountain Corps generals wore either the horn or the general's 'sunburst' badge, or sometimes both. This officer wears the regulation plus-fours, puttees and brown boots, though climbing boots and white ankle socks were also seen. Other ranks wore the standard M1939 tunic with mountain plus-fours and had no beret badge.

G3: Alpino (Private), Italian 9th Alpini, late 1942

As experienced and respected mountain infantry the Alpini Corps had been earmarked for the German advance into the Caucasus, where their skills would have been at a premium, and they were accordingly equipped as illustrated with windproof parkas and trousers. When they were diverted to serve with the Italian 8th Army on the Don in an ordinary infantry rôle their special clothing, though still inadequate for a Russian winter, did at least offer greater protection than the greatcoats of the ordinary infantry. The hat bears the famous Alpini cap badge worked in black rayon, with a gold regimental number in the centre boss. It was worn by all ranks below general officer. It is believed that rank insignia were not worn on the parka. Noteworthy is the particularly Italian arrangement of the ammunition pouches. The boots were specially reinforced for climbing. The men of the 'Julia' Division and one regiment of the 'Tridentina' managed to obtain the warmer and more practical Russian 'valenkij', or felt boots.

H1: Szakasvezetö (Lance-Sergeant), Hungarian 'Szent László' Division, 1945

'Szent László' commemorated the victorious medieval king, Saint Ladislas I. Formed on 20 October 1944, it quickly gained a superb fighting reputation. It was made up of drafts from other units and Levente Youth volunteers, formed around the élite Parachute Battalion, which seems only to have operated as infantry. The division was equipped by the Germans, and this paratrooper has a distinctly German appearance. He wears the standard field uniform, though paratroopers also had a knee-length camouflaged jump-smock. His field cap lacks the normal brown rank chevron, by now a common practice in the field. By 1944 the peaked 'Carpathian' field cap was also being widely worn. Buttons are brown for junior NCOs and men, and his 'wings' identify him as a trained paratrooper. The distinctive Hungarian trouser-breeches and footwear have given way to plain trousers and marching boots, the latter possibly German. His weapon is the Hungarian 43M sub-machine gun.

H2: Maior (Major), Rumanian Guards Cavalry Regiment, early 1941

This officer wears the modified M1930 officers' service dress with Guards distinctions and the black facings of his regiment. The M1939 cap had a wider crown, narrower hat band and smaller cap badge than previous models. The black chin strap is edged with gold, and the cap badge is the wreathed crown of the Guards. Contrary to some post-war sources the shoulder straps were not pointed, but rectangular in shape with rounded upper corners. They are in the facing colour and bear brass rank bars. The Guards cuff patch has three embroidered buttonholes but only two buttons, and the aiguillettes are gold. High on the right breast is the Staff College badge. The riding boots were plain for this regiment, without the more usual hussar bosses. The other Guards regiments, the Palace Guard and the 'Mihai Viteazul' Regiment, wore white and yellow facings respectively. In 1941 the shoulder straps were changed to khaki and the rank stripes to thin gold braid. The Guards lost their cuff patch buttons and adopted yellow aiguillettes, and the Guards

National tank markings observed among German satellite troops; there was a fair amount of variation in details of presentation. (Top) Finland, early and late patterns. Black or dark blue, shadowed white; carried on turret sides, rear, and roof, and often on hull front and/or rear plates. The tanks, mostly captured Soviet types, were variously camouflaged over the basic dark green—with ochre stripes in summer, or with light grey and brown random stripes. (See Vanguard series, nos. **14**, *The T-34 Tank*, **and 24**, *Soviet Heavy Tanks*, **published by Osprey.**) (2nd row) Hungary, pre- and post-1942: red cross edged with white on green, and white cross on black, respectively. Painted on superstructure sides. Vehicles variously camouflaged with green, brown, ochre. (3rd row) Rumania: white outline cross painted forward on superstructure sides, and repeated on engine deck, on basic olive green finish. (Bottom) Slovakia, pre- and post-1942: white cross, and white-red-blue shield, respectively. Carried on turret sides. Early vehicles camouflaged in green, brown and sand, later examples in German grey or dark yellow.

Cavalry changed to the cherry red facings of the cavalry branch.

H3: Camicia nera Scelta (Lance-Corporal), Italian Blackshirts, 1942

This dejected member of the Fascist Militia (MVSN) wears the 'War Uniform' prescribed in June 1940 for all ranks, affording little protection from the bitter winter weather. The helmet is the Army's M1933 model with the black stencilled 'Ordinary Militia' badge. Off-duty a black fez or forage cap was worn. His greatcoat is army issue with a white fasces on the standard black double collar 'flames', and he has 1940-type red rayon rank chevrons. Under the greatcoat he wears the Army tunic and plus-fours with distinctive ankle socks, often white. Officers below general rank wore basically the same uniform with small yellow rayon cuff rank insignia and silver collar fasces. Apart from the insignia the only specifically MVSN items are the black shirt and tie, but because of supply difficulties these were often replaced by the Army's grey-green. Army equipment is worn with the Blackshirt dagger. The Italian Croat Legion wore similar uniforms with Croat armshields on the left arm.

Notes sur les planches en couleur

A1 Veste d'été de campagne gris clair typiquement élimée; notez le grade sur les pattes d'épaules et l'absence de pièces de col. Notez la distinction de destructeur de tank finlandaise sur la manche. A part ce modèle M1935 de casque allemand, les Finlandais utilisaient aussi des casques tchèques, hongrois, italiens et suèdois. L'arme est une mitraillette Suomi. **A2** Uniforme de campagne règlementaire de 1936, avec l'insigne de l'artillerie sur les pattes d'épaules et les pièces de col rouges et noires de l'artillerie, avec le grade en doré. **A3** Uniforme de petite tenue, réservée aux officiers supérieurs en temps de guerre. Les culottes de cheval d'uniforme ordinaire et casquette de combat devinrent plus courants que les modèles illustrés ici dans les années qui suivirent.

B1 La tenue illustrée ici semble avoir remplacé l'uniforme d'été hongrois d'avant-guerre, y compris les pantalons longs de cheval et le crochet à l'arrière du casque M1938. Notez les détails typiquement nationaux. **B2** Tenue de campagne d'officier que seule l'ommission de ganses aux pièces bleu clair de col de la cavalerie distinguait de la tenue ordinaire. Ces pièces devinrent bleu foncé en octobre 1942 pour la nouvelle section 'mobile'. **B3** On voit ici une forte influence impériale austro-hongroise.

Un survivant de la 20ème Division, bloquée à Stalingrad. Les peaux de mouton noires ou blanches étaient utilisées pour la casquette caractéristique roumaine. **C2** Notez le calot de campagne typiquement roumain; les bottes de cavalerie; l'insigne de grade sur les pattes d'épaules, et la mitraillette Orita M1941. **C3** Uniforme de campagne modifié M1941 d'officier, avec des médailles allemandes et roumaines, le casque hollandais et les pièces de col bleu foncé de l'infanterie.

D1 Uniforme de campagne d'hiver avec pièces de col jaunes de la cavalerie. Le casque M1934 avec une bande peinte en bleu avec la croix slovaque pour éviter d'être confondu avec le casque soviétique. **D2** Encore essentiellement tchèque de style, cet uniforme a de nouvelles modifications—l'insigne de grade au col et le simple cordon d'épaule rappellent le style impérial. **D3** Elégant uniforme de campagne porté en tenue ordinaire à l'arrière des premières lignes. La baguette d'argent le long de la pièce de col indique deux ans de service; l'insigne de poitrine est celui de la Division Motorisée.

E1 On portait de nombreuses variantes de bottes de ski et de cominaisons d'hiver: ces bottes sont d'influence lapone. Un seul insigne sur le calot. **E2** Notez la forme traditionnelle en 'fer de lance' des pièces de col; après Octobre 1942, les cyclistes ont porté le bleu des troupes motorisées plutôt que le vert de l'infanterie. **E3** De même que le col en 'langue de feu' noir bordé de rouge, la cravate rouge était particulière à ce regiment. L'uniforme est 'gris officier' avec le grade en jaune à la manchette et la croix noire de la Maison de Savoie sur le casque.

F1 Notez la forte influence italienne de cet uniforme. **F2** Notez la jugulaire et le passepoil noir des unités blindées sur le calot. On épinglait parfois des cocardes de grade sur le col de la veste. **F3** Le béret, sans insigne pour les soldats et les sous-officiers, était remplacé au combat par le casque de tank français M1923, peint en bleu foncé.

G1 Ce type d'unité avait des casquettes à visière fixe; un insigne en cor de chasse à la casquette et un insigne 'aigle' sur la poitrine. L'insigne triangulaire, seulement sur la manche gauche, identifiait un sous-officier de carrière. **G2** Encore le cor de chasse sur la casquette, mais fond vert; le béret de campagne était khaki et celui de la tenue ordinaire gris cendre. Seuls les officiers portaient des insignes à la casquette. **G3** La *parka* règlementaire russe était portée sans insignes. L'insigne des Alpins, avec le numero '9' doré de ce régiment, était porté sur le calot par tous les grades.

H1 L'insigne allé de poitrine identifie un parachutiste; Bien qu'ils n'aient combattu que dans l'infanterie, ils avaient acquis une excellente réputation. L'uniforme ressemble maintenant au style allemand. L'arme est une mitraillette hongroise 43M. **H2** Tenue ordinaire M1930 d'officier avec les signes distinctifs de la Garde et les revers noirs de ce régiment. Plus tard, en 1941, la cavalerie de la Garde adopta les revers rouge cerise de la cavalerie; les pièces de manchettes des boutons disparurent et les aiguillettes dorées devinrent jaunes. **H3** Tenue basée sur celle de l'armée italienne, mais avec des pièces de col noires en double 'langue de feu' et *fasces* blancs, des chevrons rouges de grade sur les manches et la dague MVSN.

Farbtafeln

A1 Typisch schäbige, hellgraue Sommer-Feldjacke; bemerke den Rang an den Schulterklappen und das Fehlen der Kragenspiegel. Bemerke das finnische Panzerzerstörer-Auszeichnungsabzeichen am Ärmel. Ausser dem deutschen M1935 Helm benutzten die Finnen auch tschechische, ungarische, italienische und schwedische Helme. Die Waffe ist die Suomi Maschinenpistole. **A2** 1936er Vorschrifts-Felduniform mit dem Artillerieabzeichen auf den Schulterklappen und den rot und schwarzen Kragenspiegeln der Artillerie mit goldenen Rangauszeichnungen. **A3** Ausgehuniform, in Kriegszeiten auf die höheren Ränge beschränkt. Einfache Uniformreithosen und eine Feldmütze wären üblicher gewesen, als die Arten, die hier abgebildet sind, später an im Krieg.

B1 Die abgebildeten Kostüme scheinen die ungarische Vorkriegssommeruniform an der russischen Front abgelöst zu haben. Bemerke die typischen nationalen Merkmale, einschliesslich der Hosen—Reithosenkombination und der Halteklammer an der Rückseite des M1938 Helmes. **B2** Offiziersfeldkleidung—die sich von der Alltagsdienstkleidung nur dadurch unterschied, dass einige der Paspelierungseinzelheiten von den hellblauen Kavallerie-Kragenspiegeln weggelassen wurden. Im Oktober 1942 wurden diese für die neue 'mobile' Abteilung dunkelblau. **B3** Starker kaiserlich österreichischungarischer Einfluss ist hier zu sehen.

C1 Ein Überlebender der 20. Division, bei Stalingrad in die Falle gegangen. Beide, schwarze und weisse Schaffelle wurden für die charakteristische rumänische Mütze benutzt. **C2** Bemerke die typische rumänische Feldmütze; Kavalleriestiefel; Rangabzeichen an den Schulterklappen; und M1941 Orita Maschinenpistole. **C3** Modifizierte M1941 Offizies-Felduniform mit deutschen und rumänischen Auszeichnungen, holländischem Helm und dunkelblauen Infanterie-Kragenspiegeln.

D1 Winterfelduniform mit gelben Kavallerie-Kragenspiegeln. Der M1934 Helm hat einen blau gemalten Streifen und das slowakische Kreuz hinzugefügt, um eine Verwechslung mit dem russischen Helm zu vermeiden. **D2** Grundlegend noch ein tschechischer Uniformstil, zeigt dies einige neue Merkmale; Kragenrangabzeichen und einzelne Schulterkordel erinnern an kaiserliche Moden. **D3** Elegante Felduniform als Dienstuniform hinter der Kampflinie getragen. Der silberne Riegel an der hinteren Kante des Kragenspiegels zeigt zwei Jahre Dienstzeit an; das Brustabzeichen den Dienst in der 'Mobile' division.

E1 Es wurden viele Stilarten der Schneestiefel und Schneeüberanzüge getragen; diese Stiefel zeigen lappländischen Einfluss. Das einzige Abzeichen ist das an der Mütze. **E2** Bemerke die traditionelle 'Speerspitzen'—Form der Kragenspiegel; nach Oktober 1942 trugen die Radfahrer das Blau der fahrenden Truppen anstelle des Infanterie-grün. **E3** Die rote Kravatte war eine regimentale Eigenart, sowie auch die Kragen 'Flamme' in schwarz mit rot eingefasst. Die Uniform ist in 'offiziersgrau', mit gelben Ärmelaufschlagsrangabzeichen und das schwarze Kreuz des Hauses Savoy auf dem Helm.

F1 Bemerke den starken italienischen Einfluss an dieser Uniform. **F2** Bemerke den Kinnriemen und die schwarze Paspelierung der Panzertruppen an der Schiffchenmütze. Rangrosetten wurden manchmal an die Jackenkragen gesteckt. **F3** Im Kampf wurde das Beret, das für Truppen und Unteroffiziere kein Abzeichen hatte, durch den französischen M1923 Panzerhelm, dunkelblau angemalt, ersetzt.

G1 Dieser Einheitstyp hatte Mützen mit festem Schirm; ein Waldhorn-Mützenabzeichen; und ein Adler-Brustabzeichen. Das dreieckige Armelabzeichen, nur am linken Arm, lässt einen Berufsunteroffizier erkennen, anstelle eines Wehrpflichtigen. **G2** Wiederum wird ein Waldhornabzeichen getragen, auf einem grünen Tuchspiegel; das Beret war khakifarben für die Feldkleidung, aschgrau für die Dienstkleidung. Nur Offiziere trugen Mützenabzeichen. **G3** An dem 'Parka', russischen Dienst, wurden keine Abzeichen getragen. Das Alpini-Abzeichen mit der '9' in Gold für dieses Regiment wurde von allen Rängen an der Mütze getragen.

H1 Das geflügelte Brustabzeichen identifiziert einen Fallschirmspringer; obwohl sie nur als Infanterie kämpften, errangen sie einen guten Ruf. Die Uniform hat nunmehr ein deutsches Aussehen. Die Waffe ist die ungarische 43M Maschinenpistole. **H2** M1930 Offiziers-Dienstkleidung mit Garde-Auszeichnungen und den schwarzen Besätzen dieses Regiments. Später im Jahr 1941 wechselte die Garde-Kavallerie zu den kirschroten Besätzen der Kavallerie über; sie verloren ihre Ärmelaufschlagsspiegelknöpfe und die goldenen 'anguillettes' wechselten zu gelb. **H3** Grundsätzlich italienische Armeekleidung, jedoch mit schwarzen Doppelflammen-Kragenspiegeln, die weisse 'fasces' tragen und rote Rangwinkel an den Armeln, und den MVSN Dolch.